ISLINGTON

Please return this item on or before the last date stamped below or you may be liable to overdue charges. To renew an item call the number below, or access the online catalogue at www.islington.gov.uk/libraries. You will need your library membership number and PIN number.

06·14

Islington Libraries

020 7527 6900 **www.islington.gov.uk/libraries**

D1343694

ISLINGTON LIBRARIES

3 0120 02614670 4

He TeXted

The ultimate guide to decoding guys

From the creators of
HeTexted.com

CENTURY

Published by Century 2014

2 4 6 8 10 9 7 5 3 1

Copyright © He Texted Inc. 2014

Lisa Winning and Carrie Henderson McDermott have asserted their right under the
Copyright, Designs and Patents Act 1988 to be identified as the author of this work

Every effort has been made to contact the copyright holders.
The publishers will be glad to correct any errors or omissions in future editions.

This book is a work of non-fiction based on the life, experiences and recollections of
the author. In some limited cases names of people, places, dates, sequences or the detail
of events have been changed [solely] to protect the privacy of others. The author
has stated to the publishers that, except in such minor respects not affecting the
substantial accuracy of the work, the contents of this book are true.

This book is sold subject to the condition that it shall not,
by way of trade or otherwise, be lent, resold, hired out,
or otherwise circulated without the publisher's prior
consent in any form of binding or cover other than that
in which it is published and without a similar condition,
including this condition, being imposed
on the subsequent purchaser

First published in Great Britain in 2014 by
Century
Random House, 20 Vauxhall Bridge Road,
London SW1V 2SA

www.randomhouse.co.uk

Addresses for companies within The Random House Group Limited can be found at:
www.randomhouse.co.uk

The Random House Group Limited Reg. No. 954009

A CIP catalogue record for this book
is available from the British Library

ISBN 9781780892078

The Random House Group Limited supports the Forest Stewardship Council® (FSC®),
the leading international forest-certification organisation. Our books carrying the FSC
label are printed on FSC®-certified paper. FSC is the only forest-certification scheme
supported by the leading environmental organisations, including Greenpeace.
Our paper procurement policy can be found at:
www.randomhouse.co.uk/environment

MIX
Paper from
responsible sources
FSC® C016897

Printed and bound by CPI Group (UK) Ltd, Croydon, CR0 4YY

"For Susan Littlefield who told me to never give up, while supporting me through everything I ever hoped for. Vanessa Goddevrind, for proving such an inspiration to live every day. And Carrie, the most loyal business partner."

—Lisa

"To my parents, for their unwavering love and support. My husband, for being the happiest thing to happen in my life. My top tier, for being the kind of friends you only find in movies. And to Lisa, for making everything possible (and fun)."

—Carrie

contents

introduction

"what does THAT mean?"

This is the sentence that started it all. I've heard it in many languages, on several continents. Wherever my travels have taken me—from my birthplace of Sydney, Australia, to Europe, Asia, and the Americas—women are always talking about men and relationships, and their bafflement with what men say, do, and, especially, text.

By the way, this is **Lisa.**

Obtuse male texting is a global phenomenon, a growing *crisis*, sort of like climate change. Social scientists are united in their belief that men, in their digital interactions with women, are tough little buggers to figure out.

A couple of years ago, I was living in a duplex in SoHo. I was new to New York City, and I was invited to a dinner party with a bunch of American girls I sort of knew. The guests were from different professions and backgrounds. I was a bit worried as to what we'd talk about, but I shouldn't have been. Before the host cleared away the cheese plates, we'd all taken out our phones and were showing each other confounding texts from guys. We traded dating stories and played out the scenarios ("If he texted *this*, he must mean *that*, so you should reply with *this* . . . or *that*?"). It went on for hours. Whenever the conversation turned to other subjects, it always came back around to men and the mysteries of their bizarre mixed signals. And here's the amazing part: It never got boring. Never, ever, ever.

I realized I could make fast friends with any woman if I brought up the subject of men and texting. Her face would light up and the phones would come out. The manicurist. The stylist. The colleague at a business lunch, or the chick seated next to me on a plane. Even women in the buttoned-up field of banking, the type you'd think would be more sensible and not spend time deciphering a five-word text from some guy she met at a conference last week, would whip out their devices, scroll, scroll, scroll, show me the screen and ask the eternal question . . .

"what the hell?"

As important as "What the hell?" might be, the deeper question is, *Why* are we saying, "What the hell?" all the time? It doesn't matter how successful, beautiful, or accomplished you are as a person and human being. You could have single-handedly fed starving children in Africa, won an Oscar for sound editing, or built a scale model of the Eiffel Tower in your garage using empty cans of Diet Coke. But if a guy you like hasn't texted, those insecure, uncertain feelings from junior high come roaring right back. Should you text him? What should you say? How will he interpret *your* message? If he ever replies, what does it mean if it's really short, or only with an acronym or shortened form of a word (aka an abbreve), or a bizarre link to a wildlife refuge for chimpanzees? (I wouldn't be too optimistic about that last one.)

I started compiling a list of reasons why digital communications are so damn confusing.

No tone. The human elements of tonal inflection and facial expression are removed. Sure, you can try to get a sense of his emotion from the typing, the speed and frequency of his replies, if he "likes" your status update . . . or doesn't. Passing around the phone to show your friends his texts is the modern equivalent of playing back his answering machine message, looking for signs to his true feelings in the way he said, "How's it *going*?" Or "*How's* it going?" Or "How's *it* going?" Well, we don't have tone anymore. We have text. Nuances are lost. With so little to go on, every single word—every single letter—can be scrutinized endlessly. Maybe we wouldn't spend so much time on it if we didn't take a perverse kind of pleasure in analyzing it for meaning. A man's confusing text is a puzzle we're perpetually one piece away from solving.

No connection. Most women want to have meaningful, stable relationships. When we conduct our lives online, with texts and on Facebook, relationships seem fleeting, tenuous, and fake. We desire a real human connection, but the tools we use to find and establish them are mechanical. Texts don't really exist. Well, they exist, of course. But they're not letters in your mailbox, or even printed-out e-mails. You can't hold a text. You can hold your phone that the text appears on. But you're always at least one step removed from the message. Being one step removed is a subtle separation. It might play out subconsciously. But it is there.

No transparency. Anyone who uses Facebook understands the phoniness on social media, where exclamation points, humblebrags, and heart emojis rule. In the real world—the fuzzy place you slog through between stints spent staring into a computer screen—fifteen smiley faces in a row aren't as easy to come by. Is anyone really honest online? There's a lot of sugarcoating. Every meal can't really be the Best. Meal. Evah!!!!! I don't think people set out to exaggerate or sugar-coat online. But personalities shift when you type instead of talk. When interactions are pushed through the wink filter of Facebook, there is a distortion in the force. You can fall in love with someone online, then meet him and think, *He's not the same guy.*

No history. Social media and texting are relatively new for most people. Women over thirty didn't grow up with Facebook and Twitter and Snapchat. Forty-year-olds didn't even have cellphones when they started dating. When they waited by the phone, it was attached to a plug in a freakin' wall. People in their fifties are completely clueless. My mother signs her texts "Love, Mom." In movies from as recently as ten years ago, characters would come home from work, push the button on their cassette-tape answering machines, and hear, "You have no messages"—movie shorthand for "You are lonely." Sad-sack buttons don't exist anymore. Even the concept of loneliness has changed. No one is ever alone anymore, when thousands of misanthropic Reddit trolls are accessible anytime in the universe inside the phone in your hand.

No rest. In Jane Austen's day, people would write letters that could take weeks to arrive. And then weeks would go by before the reply was received. In the meantime, Lizzie and Darcy were living their lives, gardening and sewing, fencing and acquiring art. Everything played out in slow motion. Then phones entered the picture, and the pace of courting sped up and intensified. Texts have created light-speed relationships. You can send a message and get a reply in seconds. Immediacy creates intensity—or a false sense of it. Also, without forced reflective periods between communications—like exchanging letters—you're a lot more likely to type something on the spur of the moment that you will regret another moment later. We're the instant-gratification generation. We text before we think.

No relief. Voice-mail messages or even e-mail replies used to be something you'd wait for. There was a little suspense. You'd be at work or out with friends and wonder, *Did he call?* When you got home, you'd rush to see the blinking red light on the answering machine. Coming home to no messages could be very crushing. But it was just a single moment of disappointment—or exultation, if you got that call. Nowadays, with phone in hand 24/7, we exist in a constant low hum of anxiety. We don't know from one text—which could come in any second—to the next if we're being rejected, played with, or adored. Our emotions are linked to the home screens of our phones. If we get feedback, we're happy. If we don't, we freak out. It's like an addiction, with shorter and shorter spans of feeling okay between hits. Our emotions cycle much faster, too. The old-fashioned "Did he call?" is now "It'sbeenteminu tesalreadywhyhasn'thetextedback?"

While waiting to hear from a new guy, a friend of mine can't sit through a movie without checking her phone every five minutes. She gets obsessed and won't turn her phone off or put it in her bag. Her background photo is a group shot with friends on a beach. But being able to see it means there isn't a text alert blocking it. She's come to associate that fun day on the beach with the sand-in-an-open-wound feeling of not being texted by a crush. The phone is never out of sight; her anxiety is never out of mind. When a guy finally does text and she has something real to freak out about, she becomes an absolute basket case. She might be an extreme example. But I don't think so. We all check and recheck for alerts. Maybe not every five minutes, but a lot more than once a day when we get home from work.

Our cell phones are romantic minefields. How do we navigate safely through them? There are seventeen different ways to hear from a guy at any given time, and just as many ways of being rejected by him. Focusing on "What do I do if he calls?" is as quaint as waiting for the Pony Express to arrive. Now we have to contend with what to do if he tweets, Instagrams, Facebook messages, or texts? What if he wants to Skype at 2 A.M.? Is that the virtual equivalent of a Booty Call, or does he just miss your face?

After one more lunch spent discussing texts and trying to get other friends on the phone, sending screenshots of text windows to each other, I thought, *This would be so much easier if the guy's text were posted on a website. Then we could all weigh in in one place and comment on each other's comments. We could even vote on whether he was into her or not, to get a consensus opinion about confusing texts from guys.*

It would be hilarious to post text exchanges between men and women on some website for friends, and even strangers, to weigh in on—not to mention extremely helpful.

Someone really should set that up, I thought.

That was my aha moment. I had nothing to lose. "Someone" could be me. I'd build a website myself. I had no idea how to do that, but cluelessness has its own benefits. When you don't know what you're doing, you don't worry about doing it wrong.

✳

So while Lisa was having her epiphany and creating the broad-strokes vision for HeTexted.com, I was working at *Glamour* in the beauty department.

By the way, this is **Carrie**.

My job was basically my dream job. I had worked my butt off for it, and it was finally mine. When my friends asked how it was going at the magazine, I'd say, "It's awesome. I'm never leaving this job." Famous last words, right?

My friend Paul, the type of guy who knows everyone and loves making connections, told me I had to meet a friend of his named Lisa Winning. She was an entrepreneur, starting a web company. I did a lot of desk-side meetings at *Glamour* with publicists to talk about their products and services. It was part of my job. But this one sounded different. Lisa wasn't selling anything. She had a start-up website, still in beta (meaning, in the very early stages of development), about men and dating in the digital age. She wanted to talk about making her site *Glamour*-worthy, and how she should go about getting press when it was ready to launch. I owed Paul a favor, so I agreed to the meeting.

It was supposed to last fifteen minutes.

An hour later . . .

Lisa and I hit it off, like, instantly. Total mind meld. I understood and loved the idea of HeTexted.com right off the bat. Who wouldn't? I spent more than a healthy amount of time poring over guys' texts, too. My friends and I were constantly hunched over each other's phones reading them, and we had the aching backs to prove it.

I agreed with all her thinking about why texts are particularly confusing. But I also thought, *It's not just the technology that confuses us.* No matter what we're using to communicate, guys are still guys. They are still impossible to figure out, even when they talk directly to your face.

And women are still women. We have our moments of not making absolute sense or being completely honest with guys (or with ourselves) as well. The old romantic problems still exist. But now, they are on hyper-warp speed in our instant-gratification, feedback addiction–fueled culture.

It's amazing that anyone manages to communicate successfully at all.

Before Lisa left my office, she offered me an advisory board position at the website. At that point, HeTexted was largely theoretical. The technology was being worked out, but the beta version was a mess. There was no content and no investors. Lisa was a Big Idea generator, but she wasn't so good with the details about the tone and the style of the site. I knew a little about how to create a distinct look and tone to content.

If the HeTexted website were a person, I asked myself, *who would* she *be?*

She'd be me, I thought. The readers of this website would be exactly like me and all my friends. I could relate to the feelings and vision directly. I left work that day, envisioning what it would be like to work at a website start-up. At that point, it was nowhere. But it could be a full-fledged company, with an office full of people. I could see it. I could even see one woman at a desk in that cool office who looked exactly like me. She *was* me.

All night, I kept thinking about what I'd contribute to HeTexted, how the website should look and sound. How I'd want to use it, and organize the content. Little ideas kept bubbling up. I didn't sleep. I was way too excited.

The next day, I called Lisa. "I have to be a part of this thing," I said. "I'm going to quit my job."

"Don't!" she said. "I don't have any money. There's nothing there. I can't pay you." Lisa was shocked. We'd had only one meeting, and here I was, saying I wanted to quit a great job and give up a steady paycheck just to hop on her slow-moving train? She probably thought I was insane. Maybe I was. But I just knew this was my next move.

"I know you don't have money," I said. "But I really want to help you do this. I have savings. I can work for free. I know it'll all work out." I told her some of my ideas for the site, like the OMG text of the day. Having a stable of dudes to offer all kinds of relationship advice and respond to live questions, from "He sent me a photo of his refrigerator. WTF?" to "What should I buy my husband for his fortieth birthday?" The site could offer so much more than just texting advice, although that would be the primary focus. And of course I knew exactly how to spruce up the graphics with a pretty palette.

"Listen to me, Lisa. You can't go wrong with pink," I said.

lisa

 Of course, I wanted Carrie's help building the site. I'd been working on it alone, pushing this stone up the hill all by myself. I needed the energy infusion and all the fresh ideas. But I couldn't let her make such a drastic change. Not that I had a little money, or next to no money. I didn't have ANY money to pay her. There was actually nothing there. It was just a very simple website, practically a template, and an idea. To be honest, at our meeting, I imagined how great it would be if Carrie joined my company, but I could never ask someone to give up her job.

I said, "You can't quit. I can't pay you. Wait until I launch or until I have investors. Wait until it's stable."

She said, "No, we'll make it stable together. We'll make something of this together."

Her enthusiasm was like music to my ears. Someone really got it, so much so that she'd turn her life upside down to sign on. I tested her commitment and refused her offer for a few days. But she was very persuasive. I started to see how her confidence in the idea was going to inspire me and take the company to the next level. Eventually, I agreed. In a show of extreme gutsiness, Carrie gave her two-week notice the next day.

carrie

 Quitting *Glamour* to join Lisa's company was an incredibly impulsive decision. But once I made it, I never looked back. Lisa couldn't have gotten rid of me if she tried! Yes, it was a huge risk. But what in the start-up world isn't a risk? The idea was just so universal to me. How many times had I heard, "Oh God, he hasn't texted in two days. Does it mean our date sucked for him? Do I text and tell him I had a good time?"

Just talking about the universality of it made me feel like I wasn't just some weak girl cowering in a corner, my self-esteem hanging on whether some guy sent me a three-word text. I mean, I had a good job. I have a great group of friends. I am reasonably attractive and well educated. And yet, I was a pathetic overthinker in this area. I knew dozens, if not hundreds, of other women who were the same way. You can be a strong, accomplished, gorgeous woman and still freak out if you haven't been texted by a guy you don't even like that much.

What we didn't know: Would women be so tormented by guys' mysterious texts that they'd post the exchange on a website to be judged by strangers? If we were going to provide the Textbook on Texting, or the Ultimate Textiquette Guide for Ladies, we needed content! We needed people to air their dirty laundry for the entire Internet to comment on. Would they be willing?

Maybe. Why shouldn't women turn to the Internet for advice about this stuff? People go on WebMD and ask, "I have an oozing pustule in my arm. Am I dying?" People go to Angie's List and ask, "Should I hire the plumber with the visible butt crack?" We thought, *It can't be that much of a stretch for someone to post on our site, "He requested a picture after one date. Should I send?"* The idea took shape from there. Instead of relying on a team of WebMD doctors, our readers would be the experts. They could evaluate each other's text exchanges, choosing "He's Into You," "He's Not Into You," or "Verdict Is Still Out" and leaving comments. The poster would have a crowd-sourced consensus of what was going on with this guy. Anonymity—all caller IDs would be blacked out—guaranteed objectivity. It'd be wildly entertaining, too. Let's be honest, some text exchanges are downright humiliating. The site would give women a forum to share experience and opinions, without fear of embarrassment.

We hoped they would, anyway.

lisa

As soon as Carrie and I joined forces, everything just came together. Having another person on board made the entire enterprise seem less risky. Carrie knew exactly how to speak to an American audience, and that turned out to be crucial to the site's success. The main bonus, though, was the energy infusion. We pushed each other to get things done and make it happen.

HeTexted went from being an idea, to a partnership, to a real company, to an actual website. On our first day up and running, we had thirty-six users—my mom, Carrie's mom, and our friends. It was still private, though. We needed to keep it locked down until we got some content up there. We had to twist our friends' arms to go on and post text windows before we opened it up to the entire Internet. They came through for us.

On launch day, we went from having thirty-six people on the site to more than two hundred thousand. In eight hours.

HeTexted just blew *up*. How do websites go viral? For us, it started with a prelaunch article in *All Things Digital*, a blog about, er, all things digital. That got picked up by the *Huffington Post*, which led to coverage on Gizmodo, and it just kept rolling. The user numbers rose so fast, our software couldn't keep up. It was extraordinary and kind of overwhelming. People checked out HeTexted because it was a website that should have existed and now did. Just as we hoped, people *did* want to look at other women's texts from guys. And they weren't shy about commenting or weighing in, either.

What we noticed and loved from the get-go was the tone of the comments. They are supportive and comforting. Yes, there is plenty of the "he's not into you" type. For every girl who asks our readers, "Is he into me?" we want her to ask herself, "Am *I* into *him*?" Readers are opening up and sharing their wisdom, opinions, and learn-from-my-mistakes stories. I wish this site had existed when I was in my teens and twenties. The guys I would have blown off could fill a barn.

carrie

All manner of cray-cray situations pop up daily on HeTexted.com, either in the public forums or on the Ask a Bro private board for one-on-one attention. No question goes unanswered at Internet speed. The flow is heavy all month long at HeTexted. We love to give specific advice to readers regarding texts, but we realized that there seemed to be a call for general guidelines, too. Like, say, a guidebook, that covered every aspect of men and dating in the digital age.

There didn't seem to be any out there. How are there 953 diet books, but zero about the way we date now? Pregnant women get *What to Expect When You're Expecting*. Where is *What to Expect When You're Expecting a Goddamn Second Date*?

Uh, right here. In your hot little hands (or Kindle, or Nook). We hope *He Texted* does the same good as HeTexted. com, that it fills a hole that has been crying out, begging, weeping, to be filled.

bro my god

We provide need-based aid at HeTexted. All of our readers need help, and they get it—from each other, and from our stable of actual guys. That's right. Real! Live! Men! Just like you'd see advertised at a strip club. The big difference: Our guys are probably at least partially dressed when they take questions. We selected our Bros from the applicant pool based on their honesty, wit, and charm—three qualities we admire in a boyfriend, too.

Our Bros provide 20/20 guy sight (like insight, but with a Y chromosome) about any and all relationship, dating, and dude issues. Although they're usually in agreement about most of the sticky situations we'll unstick, not all men think *exactly* alike. That's why we chose three guys, each with his own distinct perspective, to serve as your romantic gurus.

Meet the HeTexted Brobassadors:

jared, 28

Relationship status: I'm currently single. But in the past, I've been your best friend, your boyfriend, the friend who likes you, the friend you like, the jerk who disappeared, the two-month fling that was never going to be serious, and your boyfriend's dumb friend.

Favorite qualities in a woman: Quiet confidence. The girl who wears something a little different, changes her hair every now and again, and can walk into a party of complete strangers and make a friend. Oh, and boobs.

Favorite qualities in a man: As the old saying goes, "Thinking is overrated." Socrates said that.

Chief characteristic: I like to think I'm funny. Funny like in the way that you and your friends have an inside joke that starts out hilarious, then gets repeated to death and gets annoying, and then all of a sudden gets funny again around the hundredth time. I'm funny and persistent.

What I appreciate most in my friends: My friends are honest in the most brutal and public way because it keeps any one of us from getting too high on ourselves.

What I appreciate most in a girl's friends: When they exist. I like dating a girl with her own crew that has their own history, inside jokes, and sexual misconduct. I've dated girls in the past who have absorbed my friends because they lacked their own. They were less interesting because it was like they had just dropped onto earth the minute we met.

Main virtue: I'm respectful. I say please and thank you and I'll push for third base with only a third of my strength.

Main fault: I hate being hated. This usually results in bad breakups, because I let the relationship go past the point of expiration. Getting dumped is easy; your friends take your side and nobody really asks why it happened. Dumping is hard. Someone you probably still like now hates you, and all of your friends tell you after the fact that she was hotter than they initially thought.

Dream job: One that gives me the opportunity to travel, day-drink, and have an oversize couch in front of a big television.

Dream girl's job: A job where she gets along with the people she works with. Guys can't stand listening to your complaints about people from work. We have enough trouble remembering your friends' names, never mind that "bitch Carol at reception."

Idea of happiness in a relationship: Eating way too much Chinese food together on a Sunday night then agreeing to not touch one another for a few hours with full understanding that there's nothing wrong with the relationship.

Idea of misery in a relationship: When a girl compares our relationship to her friends'. If your friend went apple picking with her boyfriend, good for them. But I'm not going apple picking to compete with them. Maybe we aren't the apple-picking type of couple. Maybe we do other things together. But you're probably not telling your friend, "Jared and I ate too much Chinese food together and then didn't touch for hours."

Romantic role models in real life: None. Do you think I sit in a bush and watch my favorite couples on Valentine's Day? In my opinion, the less we look to our left and right, the better we are in a relationship.

Favorite thing to do on a date: I love a brunch date. I think it's better for conversation. Girls can't just get a salad. There's no pressure for hooking up and there's nothing better than a good day-drink.

Least favorite thing to do on a date: Go to a club or anyplace where there are guys in fedoras. I judge most places by the number of guys in fedoras but especially a date spot. That means there are people there who want you to know they are "doing juuuust fine," which is miserable.

Screen names that turn me off: Anything that screams "girl power." Like, IDontNeedNoMan7 or AintNoChumpsSee-ingTheseLadyHumps. To me, that's a girl who doesn't have much power at all.

Screen names that make me pay attention: Anything that makes a girl sound like a normal person. Like IPoop2 or Cud-dlingRocks.

Natural talent I'd like to be gifted with: I'd like to play the piano. I just think there's nothing more badass than walking into a room and saying, "Oh, you guys have a piano?" Then playing for the rest of the night.

How I wish to be dumped: The same way someone takes off a Band-Aid. Quickly, with a dab of Neosporin.

Present romantic state of mind: I'm taking things slow. I'm not walking into the girlfriend store searching for something to fill a need. I'm walking through the mall, looking in all of the windows, waiting for someone to speak to me.

Relationship motto: "Making your way in the world today takes everything you've got. Taking a break from all your worries sure would help a lot." And if your girlfriend is singing along at this point, then things are pretty good.

brian, 27

Relationship status: I didn't have a girlfriend until college, and when I finally tricked someone into going out with me, I was too preoccupied with school and partying to pay enough attention to her. It was a rough breakup, but we ended up reconnecting as friends later on. I even gave her dating advice. The next girlfriend and I were a case of bad timing. She was still in college having a great time and I had just graduated and was stuck in an office for twenty hours a day. After that came a long single period where I met all sorts of different girls, from boring to crazy. I thought I knew all I needed to know and was prepared to only get into a relationship when it was definitely right. As it turned out, the next relationship I fell into was a mistake, and I stayed in it for too long. But now, finally, I'm in a relationship that's perfect. Hard to believe it can actually exist. My family and friends used to say that I'd never settle down. Turns out they were way off, and I couldn't be happier.

Favorite qualities in a woman: Besides the superficial ones (aka good looks), I like a girl who is funny, fun loving, easygoing, positive, genuine, treats people well, and is always honest.

Favorite qualities in a man: I hang out with one of the most eclectic and awesome group of guys on earth, but they all share one common trait: They're genuinely good people.

Chief characteristic: I give everyone a chance and treat everyone fairly, with respect.

(19)

What I appreciate most in my friends: Loyalty and consistency. Each one adds so much in different ways. We are always there for each other.

What I appreciate most in a girl's friends: How good they are to my girlfriend, and not trying to create unnecessary drama.

Main virtue: Honesty.

Main fault: Being too trusting.

Dream job: Running my own start-up company or funding other start-ups in a venture capital role. One day, I'd like to run a safari camp in the Serengeti.

Dream girl's job: Whatever my girlfriend is doing when she reads this. Reminder: Getting me a beer right now counts as a job.

Idea of happiness in a relationship: Being the best version of yourself without having to try while constantly wanting to be better and do more for each other.

Idea of misery in a relationship: Being with a girl who tries to pressure, guilt, manipulate, or control me. Picking fights causes endless headaches, and if a girl is ever rude toward my friends or family, it is the same as slapping me in the face. Lying is completely unacceptable, whether it is about the past, present, or future. Lies never stay hidden for long and only cause more damage and hurt down the road.

Romantic role models in real life: Both sets of my grandparents, who both coincidentally met because of World War II. My mom's parents met through letters when my grandmother was asked to write to her friend's cousin who was serving in the Marine Raiders in the South Pacific. They married when he got back to the U.S. at the end of the war. My dad's parents got together when my grandfather's best friend from the Seabees (also serving in the South Pacific) introduced him to his two sisters. Though he was set up with his friend's older sister, after one date he realized that he was in love with the younger of the two.

Favorite thing to do on a date: Go to any restaurant with good food and good drinks. Not cheap, but nothing extravagant.

Least favorite thing to do on a date: Coffee. Ugh.

Screen names that turn me off: Anything that has "hot," "qt," or "XoXo" in it. Sorry, girls, in a few years you'll look back and thank me.

Screen names that make me pay attention: Something that includes the girl's name, because no one wants to Gchat the wrong person.

Natural talent I'd like to be gifted with: The ability to be good with languages. As it stands, I can barely speak English.

How I wish to be dumped: I'd like to be told she was just going to dump me, right after I told her, "I'm breaking up with you."

Present romantic state of mind: Smitten.

Relationship motto: When I was single, my grandmother used to say: "Don't let any girls tie you down. You're too young for that; you need to see what's out there." Now that I'm a little older and more experienced, it's changed to: "Never settle for anything less than you deserve, and get out of any situation in which you're treated poorly. The right person for you is out there—it sometimes just takes time to find her."

kenny, 28

Relationship status: In high school and college, I was never the Player type, but I had a few girlfriends throughout. At the end of college I was trying to set up my friend with a girl and wound up taking her out myself (whoops!). Turned out she was the One. Several years later, I married her.

Favorite qualities in a woman: Intelligence, sass, beauty.

Favorite qualities in a man: Kindness, being dynamic, independence.

Chief characteristic: I'm levelheaded. I almost never get ruffled, so I see the root cause of a situation and how to best respond to it from a rational, Spock-like point of view.

What I appreciate most in my friends: I like "good guys." They're friendly, loyal, and treat people right.

What I appreciate most in a girl's friends: *No drama*. If a girl has a bunch of friends who love to stir up the drama, that negative tendency is someday going to find its way into your relationship. If her friends are cool and collected, it's a great sign that your girl is, too.

Main virtue: Dependability. I'm the Maytag of men.

Main fault: Sloppiness. I can't help it! I could be standing in the middle of it, but I just don't see the mess.

Dream job: Internet tycoon.

Dream girl's job: President.

Idea of happiness in a relationship: The kind of connection where everything just clicks. It's not about checking off a list of things you want in a girl or a relationship. You're always going to be disappointed if you operate that way. The right person makes you forget you ever had a list.

Idea of misery in a relationship: Drama, drama, drama.

Romantic role models in real life: My parents. They're still happily married after thirty-one years. They are great examples of putting the other person first and taking time to realize that most of the issues that they're feeling are due to their own baggage, not the other person.

Favorite thing to do on a date: Ice skating. It's romantic, fun, and exciting, and girls associate that exhilaration with you. It's always a win.

Least favorite thing to do on a date: Go to the movies. Why do people do this on a first, second, or third date? You can't talk to each other or see each other in natural light, and you run the risk of hating each other's taste. Plus, you run into all those awkward "do we hold hands?" scenarios.

Screen names that turn me off: Any that alternate capitals and lowercase letters LiKeThIs, especially if it contains the words *HoTcHiCa*.

Screen names that make me pay attention: Anything clever.

Natural talent I'd like to be gifted with: Rap battling skills.

How I wish to be dumped: A song-and-dance number would be fun. Short and sweet, though. Don't drag it out.

Present romantic state of mind: Married for life!

Relationship motto: If the shoe doesn't fit, don't wear it for more than a couple months.

*

As you can see, each Bro has a unique and distinct flavor. We think of Jared as a Classic Bro—as he describes himself, "just the right amount of douchebag." He calls 'em like he sees 'em—usually through beer goggles. He's single, and likely to stay that way for a while. Brian is a nice guy, a romantic in a new relationship. Despite being smitten, he manages to retain his male objectivity. Kenny is a married mensch, a pragmatist, and a classic wit. Full disclosure: Kenny was so gifted at responding to our readers' questions, we decided to promote him to King of Bros. That's his official title.

So, if you'd like, decide on your favorite to follow throughout the book. Or follow all three. Or pick two and unfollow one. It's not like Twitter. He'll never know. You can stalk our Bros in confident anonymity. They, on the other hand, are out there, completely exposed, using their real names and photos. Our Bros have nothing to hide and no reason to lie. Take their word as the unvarnished, absolute truth as they see it.

(1)

he friended

He added you as a Friend on Facebook!
Does that mean he wants to be your
boyfriend in real life?

the context

You meet a guy at a party or bar. The next day, he sends you a Friend request. An alternate scenario: You have mutual friends, and he came across your profile while clicking around the ultimate time suck that is Facebook. He impulsively sent you a request. Level-one contact initiated. Now what?

If nothing more, Facebook has become the way people connect, learn about each other, and start the conversation that, with time and good luck, can turn into a full-fledged love relationship. Or not. Friending (attention, *Oxford English Dictionary*, we've got a new word for you) is the digital equivalent of an introductory handshake at a business lunch, a "'Sup?" at a backyard barbecue, or a "You went to college with Camille, right?" at an apartment party. It's empty and meaningless . . . unless it isn't.

The guy has to have been curious about you to make the request. Effort was made. Attention was paid. That has to mean *something*.

the subtext

carrie

The old-school conventional wisdom (wake up, Grandma!) was that it's always a good idea to be friends with a guy before you get romantically involved. Okay, we get that. Before you go home with a dude, you should have some idea of what kind of person he is with his clothes on. But does new-school conventional wisdom say it's a good idea to be Facebook Friends before you hook up? That's a little bit more complicated.

Let's say you meet a cute guy at a party. Naturally, the first thing you do when you get home from the party is Google his name, then slog through his Facebook, Twitter, Instagram, YouTube, Tumblr, and Pinterest accounts. You can learn as much about this man in a one-hour search as your mother did about your dad during twenty years of marriage.

That's a marvel of the Internet age, right? Hold the iPhone. You do not want to be the woman who knows too much. How annoying would it be on your first date to know the answers to every question? You can't very well ask with sincerity, "So, do you have siblings?" if you've already seen photos of his sister's wedding. But you have to ask out of politeness. Hope you're as good at acting as you are at Googling.

What if you knew for a fact that he'd seen you in a bikini before the first kiss. How would you feel? Like you're a swimsuit model, or like he's a creep?

Depending on how attracted you are to this guy (and you can't be really, really into him yet since you don't really, really know him), you could take his Friending as a good sign. He wasn't satisfied by what he turned up on Google, like that video on YouTube of your valedictory speech at high school graduation with the jaunty tilt of your mortarboard. He wants to see more, like what's under the black gown.

So you accept the request. Now he can see the photos of your trip to the Bahamas, and you can read about his years as a college DJ. He has a sense of humor. So do you. You probably like the same movies, books, and TV shows. You can picture yourselves on the couch watching *Game of Thrones* together for years and years to come.

Just like that, things have gotten ahead of themselves.

A lot of women on HeTexted complain that they had such high hopes for a new relationship and don't understand how it went so wrong so fast. I blame the false sense of connection you get on Facebook. If we have too much info going in, we don't get to settle into the getting-to-know-each-other stage and establish a real connection. Facebook is not (always) your friend. It can betray you by providing way too much info about you before the relationship gets off the ground.

lisa

Armed with so much material, we women, with our wonderful imaginations, can write chapter and verse about what a relationship with a new crush could be. In our heads, we construct seduction scenes and funny dialogue. We fall in love with our main characters, our romantic heroes, and plot out the beginning, middle, and happy ending of the story . . . before the relationship has played out in real life.

Every woman is a novelist.

I do this constantly and usually end up

embarrassed. One example: I met a guy in New York. We went on a date and kissed once. It was a solid, long kiss. I wouldn't humiliate myself over just a peck. I have some dignity! Like an idiot, I got it in my head that the kiss meant we had a future together. I envisioned this future, our four-day weekends in Vermont, and all the breakfasts we'd make in our pajamas. I stalked him innocently on Facebook, sifting through his photos and witty updates. I started to send him messages regularly. "I bet you like your eggs scrambled, don't you?" Cheeky things like that. In hindsight, I see his terse replies for what they were: polite but detached. I hadn't let it go so far in my head that I'd split Thanksgiving and Christmas visits between our families. But I did get swept away by the vision of what we could have meant to each other someday. He didn't make any effort to see me again. Eventually, I woke up to the truth. I fell in love with a story about what could have been, and that made me misread the signals. He wasn't into me at all.

carrie

I searched my husband's name the night we met. Google turned up only basic biographical info. His Facebook Wall was blocked to non-Friends. I couldn't access anything. Woof. (He ended up adding me a short while later.) I think it was for the best not to see his Wall, though. We got to know each other in real life, instead of thinking we'd gotten to know each other based on our online personas.

If a dude adds you as a Friend, he's not necessarily drooling for you, but he is, at the least, feeling friendly toward you. We ladies are naturally curious creatures. Our impulse to learn more combined with our lightly harnessed imaginations can lead us to take a Facebook Friendship and run with it. We'll run so far and so fast, we'll outpace the relationship as it unfolds in real time. So, to get back to the point, if you really like him, under no circumstances should he be your Friend. **,,**

so he's into me . . .
if he sends a friend request?

Bro consensus: Men and women are either friends, or more than friends. Regarding Facebook, if he were into you, he'd want to be *less* than Friends.

kenny
On HeTexted.com, women send me hundreds of e-mails looking for hidden

meaning in a guy's behavior. But the simplest, most straightforward, explanation is usually correct. With that in mind, I say with complete sincerity, that if a guy sends you a Friend request on Facebook, it is for one reason only: He wants to see you in a bikini.

He might want more than that, too. But that is the number one reason. It's superficial. Now, a friend add might mean something deeper to him, depending on circumstances. When you met, did you have a quick pass or a long conversation? Did the request come the day after you met? That same night? Timing is a big indicator of interest. A fast add could be a good sign. But if you see he's added ten friends from the same party, I wouldn't read anything into it. Remember the simple explanation. A guy who adds ten people in one night is just racking up friends. He's not using the nine other adds to obscure his ulterior motives: to get to you, and only you.

brian

I do think a Facebook add is an important move in a relationship. We knew each other for about three years before we hooked up. There was this instant attraction, but we both had someone else at the time. It became a thing, a game of who was going to make the first move and add each other as a Friend. There was an understanding that, in our situation, being Facebook Friends meant we didn't want to be just friends. On the other hand, we were in a big group, and not Friending so stridently was kind of weird, too. We were all hanging out one weekend and someone wanted to share photos or something, so we spontaneously added each other. It was kind of a letdown. I wanted to put more significance on it.

Personally, before my girlfriend, I didn't add anyone who I might get romantically involved with. I wanted them to get to know me through face-to-face interactions. I do know plenty of people who add potential hookups just to see what they look like in different situations. Casual. Dressed up. In a bikini. If she doesn't have a bikini picture, guys will wonder, *Why not?* Assumptions are made on Facebook, on both sides. He might check out what her friends look like, to see what kind of crowd she travels in. I've heard of guys looking at a girl's mother for a clue what she'll look like in thirty years. If they don't like what they see in the photos, they Unfriend without a backward click.

Some guys are dicks.

jared

I did JDate.com for a while. I started exchanging messages with one girl, and then we became Facebook Friends. I checked out her Wall and made a lot of sweeping assumptions about her that might not have been true, but the mind goes where it goes. I decided that there is room for only one person with commitment issues in any relationship, and that's me! Before we'd had a first date, I blew her off.

Friending on Facebook is entry into someone's life. You're in their virtual room—and they're in yours. I'm always tempted to have a quick look around a girl's room (especially if she's naked), but I don't want her going through my stuff. Yup, it's a double standard, one of many you'll read about in this book. I refuse to be Facebook Friends with women until we've met and have connected face-to-face for a while, say, a month or two. I want some mystery. At least give me a few days of imagining what she might look like in a bikini before I see a photo of it.

Yes, it's all about the photos. Guys are visual beings. I would look at eight hundred photos on Facebook before I read a single one of her status updates. Women should understand how guys look at photos. It's kind of like an investigation. Of course, we want to see the sexy shots. We also want to see that she's not a loser. Does she have group shots with friends? Does she go out a lot? Where are the current photos? Is her profile picture from ten years ago when she was at her attractiveness peak? Guys look for that and a million other things. Don't want your photos scrutinized? Don't Friend.

want

A guy who . . .

* Intrigues you enough to search about him on Google.

* Keeps an element of mystique by not adding you on Facebook. Smart guy. He either has experience or the wisdom to know that an avalanche of premature information could bury a potential relationship.

* Doesn't pressure you to add him on Facebook. It's not that you have anything to hide. But if he wants to get to know you, he can take you to dinner.

do not want

If you are Friends, a guy who . . .

✳ *Only* looks at the photos. What is it with their dependence on visuals? It's a miracle men can read books that don't have pictures. Ask him outright, "Did you just scroll through my photos or read my Wall?" If he stammers, you have your answer. If he says, "I read your Wall . . . to find more photos," he might not be horrible. At least he's honest.

✳ Asks stalkerish questions about things you posted more than a year ago. There's healthy curiosity, and then there's unhealthy obsession. If a guy has that much time on his hands, to read through your entire Facebook history, he should get a job before he thinks about finding a girlfriend.

autocorrect

So, you accepted his Friend request *against our stellar advice*. You can't very well Unfriend now without it becoming an issue. If you do take him on as a social media friend, put him on your Restricted List. Step-by-step instructions:

1. Go to his page.

2. Click the checked Friends box.

3. Scroll down to Add to Another List.

4. Click on Restricted.

A Restricted Friend can only see posts of yours on his news feed (if he's lucky enough to catch them), your public information (hometown, employment, status, some "likes") and profile pictures. That's more than enough for a first date.

the memo

Facebook isn't the only social media outlet for minor stalking, or, as we call it, "research." You can expect to unearth different nuggets at each site. Such as:

✳ **Twitter.** If you care what he had for lunch, then Twitter is a safe spying site for you. In a romantic soft-stalking context, it's ideal, because you can read someone's tweets without following him—as long as his feed is public. He'll never know you read his one-sentence review of *Star Trek*. The Bros tell us that him following you has zero romantic significance. In a way, being "out" as a follower would put him more in the friend category. If he really liked you, he'd read your tweets on the sly.

✳ **Instagram.** Meh. Similar to Twitter in the intimacy landscape (as barren as the surface of the moon). You can look at each other's artsy shots of sunsets and graffiti. Our Bros consider this an age-sensitive site. Young people (under-twenties) use it. The older crowd does not get it.

✳ **LinkedIn.** He doesn't want you. He wants you to hire him.

✳ **YouTube.** If you are crushing on a narcissist/musician/comedian/performance artist (God help you), a look at his channel will tell you all you need to know about whether he will expect you to split the bill on your dates.

✳ **Tumblr.** These blogs are usually just a lot of photos. Have a look. You know you will. But try not to waste a lot of time and mental energy writing your own captions for his pix.

✳ **Pinterest.** If he has a Pinterest board, you will learn one very important thing: He's a woman.

(2)

he chatted

Your main crush initiated a Facebook
chat or commented on your status.
Should you start planning your long
weekend in Vermont?

the context

Clearly you didn't take our advice to put a new man on
your Restricted List. Hey, it's your life! You do what you
want. He turned out to be a decent Facebook friend, actually. He comes up a lot lately in your notifications, "liking"
and commenting and even opening a chat window . . . to
his heart??

the subtext

carrie

When you're home and should be folding that pile of laundry, Facebook sucks you into its never-ending stream of useless information. Photos of people's kids, dogs, dinners, kids, ocean views, artsy pix of trees, kids, kids, kids. Perhaps the kids could climb up into the artsy trees and stay there for a while? Just a suggestion.

Updates can be uncomfortably political or religious ("God loves u 2day!"). They might be sadly, uncomfortably revealing ("I admit I have a problem: Only two bottles of wine in the fridge! All for me! LOL"). Ninety percent of it is fluff. But it's 100 percent addictive. Just like with a gif of puking kittens, you can't look away. And that's *before* you throw a potential relationship into the mix. Then your News Feed scrolling gets really intense.

That little *f* icon on our phones begs to be tapped. And every time you do, you're one tap closer to being *that girl*. You know who I mean. The Facebook junkie who updates with real-time commentary while watching *The Bachelor*. The girl who posts ten photos of her butt in different jeans from the fitting

room at H&M, asking for "brutal honesty."
Our honest opinion: Your trolling for com-
pliments is tiresome, and possibly psychotic.
Also, you're in love with your own butt.

lisa

If you're feeling lonely or
bored, Facebook is always
there. It should be used as a
way to pass the time. But if you use it too
often, you can become dependent, even
addicted, to it. Notifications become your
meth. Or you could see it this way. Facebook—and Twitter for that matter, where
people seem to disappear for days—is like an
alternate universe that chews up your Real
Life and spits it out into a puddle of winks,
exclamation points (henceforth "exclams"),
and optical illusion pictures that still don't
move, even after you comment on them. You
can lose perspective in there. It's a bizarre
world where a guy can "like" you without
like-liking you. He can chat you up without
actually saying a word. And he can poke you
(real good) from different time zones. When
we're crushing, we grasp at straws. We're
optimists. We eat hope for breakfast, lunch,
and dinner. Therefore, we ascribe huge significance to a "like" or a comment from a man

we're interested in. If he starts a Facebook chat with you, or retweets you, and keeps the conversation going, he must be way into you, right? If he weren't, why would he bother interacting with you on social media at all?

so is he into me . . .
if he "likes," comments, pokes, chats?

Bro consensus: Likely.

jared
A girl posted this question to HeTexted: "He keeps on poking me on Facebook, and then sent the message, 'Real life poking is also allowed.' What should I reply?"

I answered, "Tell him, 'I practice safe poking . . . unless I'm in a monogamous poke war.' Or, 'I don't poke. I have sex.'" If a girl replied that second one to me, I'd have an accident in my pants.

kenny
Yeah, I remember that question. I'd say ignore it, unless you're cool with just

a hookup. If you want more from this pokey wordsmith, just say something forward and sassy like, "Fascinating! You'll have to buy me dinner first. Like eighty times."

brian

Some guys poke and post random comments because girls like to be "liked." They *love* to be "liked." Guys are completely aware of this. They know girls take note of every comment and notification they receive. I've been out with girl friends who check their Facebook constantly and get excited about any feedback. Twenty "likes"? It makes their day. Just five "likes"? That's an update fail. So if a guy wants to get her attention and show interest, especially if the two of you are just getting to know each other, he will "like," comment, and chat just so his name is on your mind. He doesn't necessarily like what you posted, or have anything relevant to say about it. He's doing it for the sole purpose of making you notice that he's making an effort.

On the other hand, he might just genuinely like your update.

In a nutshell, if your updates are stupid and annoying and he "likes," he is into you. If your updates are witty and relevant, and he "likes," he might be into you. If he doesn't "like" your updates at all or anyone else's, he's out in the world, doing stuff, having a real life where he's meeting girls whose noses aren't glued to their phones.

Any "liking," chatting, and tweeting must lead to dating, and commenting back and forth to each other's faces. There is no substitute for actual conversation. "Liking" on Facebook is fine. It's out there, and people register it. It's public and safe. But it's just not personal. If a guy doesn't move beyond "liking" to making a plan—give it a time frame of a couple of weeks, a month max—then he's not that into you. If he really liked you, he'd reach out with a Facebook or Twitter direct message to set a date. Guys who don't might be pathologically shy, or are afraid to go offline. Is that the kind of guy you want? A serial "liker" who won't take you to dinner?

Poking, in my opinion, is for cowards.

jared

I have to bring up the reverse situation, of a girl "liking" and commenting on a guy's updates or tweets. If you're in an established relationship, "liking" is just being supportive. But if a girl I went out with once "liked" and commented on everything, I'd think there was something wrong with her. Personally, I don't want any new woman in my life to "like" or comment on my Wall at all. That's public. If she has something to say to me, she can send me a private message.

Facebook is forever. If you comment on something, it's out there for all of your friends to see. Now, say you don't like her comment. What then? You're in the awkward situation of having to delete it. She might ask, "Why did you delete my comment?" People can be clueless about Facebook etiquette. They're also clueless about what's funny. But if you delete her unfunny or just plain weird comment, then you have explaining to do. She's pissed. You're resentful. It's just a horrible situation to be in when you should be having fun and getting to know each other in the best possible light.

Think of it like this: You're standing in a field with every one you know. A "like" is the equivalent of yelling at the top of your lungs in that field, where everyone you know can hear it, "I like this!" If I went out on a date with a girl, I wouldn't want her yelling, "I like this!" to everything I said. But if she came up to me in that field and whispered in my ear, "I like this," I would definitely have a better reaction.

The tone of the new relationship should

be intimate. Private. Just between the two of you. If a girl poked me after a first date, there would not be a second. Who even pokes anymore? Did anyone, *ever*? Poking on Facebook is just as creepy as if you randomly, physically poke a stranger at a bar with your boner. I haven't done that in a long time.

kenny

What else does he "like"? If he "likes" *only* your stuff, he's definitely into you. Some guys are all over the place. They "like" everything and everyone. If you notice that he's commenting on ten girls' profile photos, then assume he's a Player. Now, chatting is a different story. Some people are capable of chatting with five different people at the same time. Younger girls tend to do this. But guys won't and don't bother. Guys have enough friends. They'd rather do just about anything than get stuck in a chat with anyone, even a girl they really like. It's like being chained to the couch, without the TV on and no beer or chips. So know that when a guy wants to chat, he's definitely exploring the possibilities.

want

A dude who . . .

✳ Is a judicious "liker." A good parameter would be to get one "like" per day OR one comment or reply tweet. After you're Friends, it'd be creepy if he didn't make his Friendship known and just stalked you in silence. You want to know he's paying attention to your online social life, and at least pretends to like what you're up to.

✳ Makes an effort with his comments. They're more than a generic "awesome!!" or "cool!!!" A tiny spark of wit or humor would be nice to see. And if he has relevant insight into your updates, so much the better.

✳ "Likes" your comments. We know that's kind of getting stuck on the feedback treadmill to hell. You comment. He "likes." You "like" his "like," until the universe collapses into itself with a giant sucking sound. Again, we're talking *occasional* "liking." Once a day or less. It's just polite. Too much, though, is creepy.

do not want

The dood who . . .

✳ Is a public wanker. He "likes" you all right, as long as it's on Facebook. You're his favorite, on Twitter. But the relationship is stalled. He won't take the next step and send you a private message. Give it a month. If he doesn't go private by then, he's either not into you or a wimp. The screen can be a buffer, or a protective shield. But is that really the kind of guy you want? Someone who hides in front of a computer screen?

✳ "Likes" your comments, but doesn't "like" or comment on your posts first. This guy is passive-aggressive. One day, you'll ask him to turn down the TV volume ten times. When you confront him, he'll say, "Oh, sorry. I didn't hear you. The TV was too loud."

✳ Chats with no clear purpose. When you're chatting or messaging, there should be a point. It's all well and good to connect. According to our Bros, guys do use chat to keep the spark alive between dates. But setting up the next dates should be the theme of the exchange. If he's not actively pushing for the next face-to-face (and we don't mean Skype or FaceTime), then why bother? You have enough Friends already.

autocorrect

✳ Don't be the girl who "likes" too much. Men are fiercely private. If his boys see some chick is popping up all over his Wall and Twitter feed, he'll feel uncomfortable and exposed. Save your likes and comments for when they count.

✳ When chatting or private messaging on Facebook, set a time limit on it. You are a busy, beautiful, in-demand woman. You've got shit to do! You can't sit around all night chatting and waiting for his next message. No matter how sizzling your textual chemistry is, keep it short. It you go longer than fifteen minutes, it'll cool off fast, believe us. If he doesn't ask you out by then, too bad. He'll speed it up next time.

✽ No matter how casual and comfortable you are on chat, do not ask him out first. He might open the chat window, and open a metaphorical door ("I've got nothing going on this weekend. Totally wide open. Free as a freakin' bird. No plans, at all. Nothing on the iCal"): DO NOT TAKE THE BAIT. He'll be turned off, even if he thinks he wants you to pull the trigger. We know it sounds old-fashioned. Yes, more women graduate college than men. Yes, 40 percent of primary bread-winners are women. Yes, the CEO of Yahoo! is a hot blonde. But the dude has to ask the girl out the first few times.

the memo

If you take away one thing from this chapter, let it be this: There's "face value," and then there's "Facebook value."

"Face value" means, basically, what you see is what you get. A person, thing, or situation genuinely is what it appears to be. The phrase actually comes from coinage. The value of a coin is imprinted on its face. A dime is a dime.

On the other hand (face), you have "Facebook value," or what you see isn't necessarily what you get. A person, thing, or situation is not necessarily what it appears to be. You can't even be sure that the person you're "liking" and chatting with is actually an adult male. Being duped on Facebook is so prevalent that "catfishing" is a common phenomenon. Now, you might know for a fact that the person whose status you're commenting on really exists and is really a human adult male. BUT his friends might've hacked into his account and started randomly (or not so randomly) posting on other people's Walls or liking comments, or even chatted. Not to make you paranoid, but this does happen. Or he's inflating himself online, or acting like a dick because his friends will see what he posts. A dime is not necessarily a dime, according to Facebook value. A jerk is probably still a jerk, though.

(3)

he texted!

You're exchanging private texts via your iPhone or CrackBerry. Texts are like Insta-Intimacygrams delivered right into your palm. Are you one text away from being his real-life favorite?

the context

You're finally off the coy romantic tenterhooks of Facebooking and tweeting, and on to an actual relationship. Exchanged "likes," LOLs, breaking news updates about what you had for lunch and fave lines from *Girls* were Internet foreplay. Well, you've taken the quantum leap to private texts, which probably means you've also been on a few dates. You might've spent some offline time with your clothes off, too. But despite the intimacy upgrade, his texts are ambivalent and confusing. He's inconsistent about replying, sometimes getting right back, and other times falling off the edge of the earth for days at a time. Sometimes, he's really brief. Not cool. Not K. It's hard to tell if he's being polite, friendly, friendly-with-benefits, or is genuinely into a relationship.

the subtext

carrie

I met my husband on a Tuesday night at a karaoke bar. I sang a rousing rendition of "You Make My Dreams Come True" by Hall and Oates. Yes, I too am surprised a dozen guys didn't immediately rush up to me. But one guy did. He said, "I'm Matt. I just wanted you to know what a terrible voice you have."

I said, "Thanks! You're a gem to tell me."

"Yeah, you're really bad," he said. "But can I buy you a drink anyway?"

He was cute. Loved his smile and brown eyes but was a little put off by the teasing. I said, "Maybe later."

"Come on, let me buy you a drink."

"You must be a big Hall and Oates fan," I said. Then I went back to my friends and hung out for another hour or so. Before we left, I said good-bye to Matt. He asked me for my number again, and I gave it to him.

I was two steps toward the bar exit when my phone vibrated. "Hello?" I asked.

"Just making sure you didn't give me a fake number," he said.

Matt sure was persistent and predictable. True to form, he texted me at 2 P.M. the next afternoon—the universally acknowledged sweet spot for getting in touch. If he'd texted earlier, it would have been too aggressive. If he'd texted later, it would have been standoffish. He was a carefully casual guy.

At the bar the night before, we'd talked about Shake Shack, a famous burger place in New York that always has lines around the block. He worked across the street from it. So the text said, "Hey. It's Matt from last night. I was wondering if you wanted to grab Shake Shack this Friday for lunch."

I was curious about Shake Shack. I'd been too intimidated by the ten-mile-long line to get in. But if he was willing to stand there and wait, fine. Most of our date would be spent standing on the street, shuffling in a queue. Super romantic! I showed up as planned on Friday, and we had a nice lunch. The line moved quickly, and I was in good company. He was very up front about his intentions and even asked me what I was doing later that night. Then he mentioned the name of a well-known bar. "I'm going there with some friends," he said. "You should come."

Having been through a few noncommittal guys in the last couple of years, my dating mantra had been, "Just give me a guy who can tell me what he wants." So when I had one in front of me, it made me happy, but I also didn't really know how to handle it. I panicked and told him I had plans, even though I didn't. I wound up staying in with a few girlfriends. We ordered a pizza and watched *Knocked Up*.

The next night, Saturday, I ran into Matt at yet another bar (no, we are not alcoholics, just enthusiastic drinkers). It was such a weird coincidence, so I bowed to fate and hung out with him all night. We had a great time and drank, uh, plenty.

On Sunday, I texted him first and said, "I had a really nice time last night. I hope you aren't too hungover. Haha."

He replied, "Haha. Yeah, not doing too well."

"Yeah, sucks."

I expected to hear back from him right away. But nothing. He didn't keep the exchange going. He just let it die. And his "not doing too well" was so generic and not personal. It was something he could have written to anyone, and didn't reference anything from the night before.

I kept my phone close all day Sunday. He never texted back. I got really worked up about it. I'd thought he liked me more than I liked him. But now, apparently, he didn't like me at all! I checked my screen every two minutes. Nothing.

By Monday morning, I'd reached a point of screen-checking mania. I was on the verge of throwing my phone through the wall. Then, at 2:00 P.M.—the Texting Hour—he wrote, "I was wondering if you'd like to have dinner on Wednesday."

I replied, "WHY DID YOU JUST CUT ME OFF LIKE THAT YESTERDAY??? WHAT'S WRONG WITH YOU??"

Just kidding.

I played it cool and wrote back, "Yeah, sounds good!" and cursed my lack of backbone.

Later on, once we were dating, I asked him about that day of silence. I confessed that I had spent the entire day mourning the death of our newborn relationship. He looked at me like I had seven heads. "I was hungover, that's all. How could you possibly read so much into that?"

Just because I was up for texting while hungover didn't mean he was. His suffering style was to lie in a dark room. Mine was to whine about my pain to all my friends. I totally misread his silence. It had nothing to do with me, or us. I freaked out for nothing. I figured he let the conversation die because he had no interest in me anymore. Instead of thinking, *He's recovering*, I thought, *He hates me! He's turned off. What did I do wrong?*

In hindsight, I'm glad it happened. Not hearing from him all day made me like him a lot more. (If you're rolling your eyes you can stop, because you KNOW that's how it goes!) He had no idea what he was doing, but it worked. I stopped being smug about how much he liked me, and let down my guard. We fell in love and got married a few years later. That one Sunday was the most panicked I've ever been over Matt. In twenty-four hours, I went from thinking I had him to feeling like I'd blown it—over literally NOTHING.

It all just proves that you can read a lot into texts (the ones you receive, and the ones you don't) that isn't actually there. We have so little to go on. To fill in the blanks—between the lines of a text, and between texts themselves—we come up with all kinds of theories for what it all means. Nine times out of ten, women go to the worst-case scenario.

> We don't give OURSELVES the benefit of the doubt.

lisa

Early-relationship texting is all about levity. In those first few weeks, you're both so worried about not coming across as too intense that it's nearly impossible to know if he takes you seriously as a potential girlfriend. The superficial tone can be exhausting to maintain, but it's a necessary frustration. If you're not super casual, he'll think you're a psycho bitch. If he's not playing it cool, you'll think he's a psycho killer. A full-court press from either side is a major turnoff. We hear women say on the site a lot of variations of, "If he'd just answer my texts in a timely manner and say how much he liked me, I'd be thrilled." Actually, you'd probably be turned off and think he was too into you. Carrie's story is a perfect example of how the subtle push-pull of texting can deeply affect your emotional response. He's the same guy, whether he sends a text or not. But how you feel about him has completely changed. It might seem like just a few lines of meaningless typing. But light little texts are actually loaded.

so he's into me . . .
if he sends me private texts?

Bro consensus: He's into you, but in what way remains to be seen.

brian

If a guy comes on strong, saying, "You're so beautiful. I really, really loved meeting you," he's just trying to get into your pants. Starting off with the head-over-heels flattery and over-the-top declarations of how much he likes you should be a red flag. If he doesn't back up the words through some sort of commitment—seeing you exclusively a few nights a week—the "you're so hot" texts are pure manipulation. I prefer the approach of keeping it light and joking around. A guy who is into you will text to make plans, not just to slobber all over you. I think Carrie's story proves it. Matt texted her only to make plans to see her. Otherwise, he didn't bother. She expected some amount of banter, and that's a valid complaint. But Matt proved his honest interest by always going for the actual date. Women like the affirmation of a few flirty text exchanges between dates. Guys, frankly, could do without it.

jared

The tone is set from your very first text exchange. If he gets back to your text within an hour, then that's the tone for the relationship from now on. If it changes from there, it has to be due to special circumstances. Such as, the dude was sick in bed, his phone was dead, or he was on an airplane. Without a good reason, a guy can't just go a day between texts if you've already established a consistent back-and-forth pace. He might make excuses ("Crazy busy!"), and girls will definitely make a million excuses for him ("He's crazy busy!"). But no matter how busy, sick, hungover, whatever, if he's into you, you will hear from him soon enough. If his feelings have dropped off, his not texting is his way of signaling the change without having to embarrass you both by actually saying, "Not feeling it." He didn't forget to text. Yes, he might be really busy at work. But if he was into you, he'd take five seconds to text. No man is so insanely inundated that he can't send a text that reads, "Can't talk now. I'll text tonight."

Granted, some people are generally bad at texting. They don't look at their phone as often as a normal person. But you'll establish those kinds of patterns and behaviors early on. A guy who's good about texting doesn't suddenly turn bad—unless it's on purpose.

kenny

The timing of a text matters. For example, if he messages right away while you're still at the party or bar, he's into you. If you don't hear from him the following day? Don't panic. If a guy likes you today, he'll like you tomorrow. He'll even like you the day after that, unless you send him fifteen texts asking, "What's going on? How are you?" Then he might reconsider.

Also, content is a good clue. It's absolutely true that a guy who flatters you and goes over the top with the sweet talk, like, "You're the most beautiful woman I've ever seen," "I can't stop thinking about you," "I'm mad attracted to you," is a Player. I guarantee you he's sending the same texts to five other women. The idea is to drop a dozen lines in the water and hope he hooks someone. It's like the Naked Man Theory from *How I Met Your Mother*. When a girl goes to the bathroom, the guy takes off all his clothes in the living room and waits for her. Either she'll run out screaming and punch him in the 'nads—or she'll take a good look at him and say, "Okay, let's go." A

Player sends out those "you so hot" texts to see if any of the girls on his contact list are good to go.

A Sub, on the other hand, is a bit more subtle with his text tone. He's light. He tries to make some jokes. He's best friends with irony. This Sub is making an effort to downplay his feelings—because he actually has some. When a guy is purposefully light, he might have deep feelings for you. But don't go digging to unearth them! A guy has to reveal himself in his own good time.

Bad textual chemistry on display. She's trying to go deep, but he's not having it.

jared

When I'm into a girl, I ask a lot of questions in texting. Then there's a compelling reason for her to reply. A text exchange stalls when neither party asks a question that requires an answer. A girl might take it as a bad sign, when in reality he just didn't have anything else to say.

Here's an idea for you women to chew on: If you don't have anything to say, don't text! It's fine to say, "What's going on?" But that's pretty lame and boring. A guy doesn't want to waste his time with bullshit, even if he's into you. He'd see replying to you as a necessary evil that comes along with the possibility of sex.

Speaking of the possibility of sex, a guy who's into you will always be moving toward a physical get-together. A little back and forth—"'Sup?" etc.—is okay, but only if it's toward making a plan. So what if you've been texting for a week, and he doesn't ask you out? You can't let him get away with just sitting on the texting fence forever. Make it clear that you want to go on a date. Do NOT ask him out. Just let him know that if he asks you, you won't shoot him down. A text like, "I'm going to a party this weekend. You and your friends should come," or, "This week is nuts, but next week is wide open. We should get together," is totally appropriate. You're creating a chance to get together without being too forward. Now he's got the ball. He has to make a date or dance a little bit to postpone. At that point, you will get your answer about whether he's into you, or if he's just keeping you on a string.

Be honest with yourself!

If a guy begs off making plans, then move on. Text, "Okay. Sounds great. Let me know." You've done all you can. The pressure is completely off your shoulders. It's all up to him. Do not text him again. People are always busy until they don't want to be. If he doesn't make time for you, the answer is obvious: He doesn't want to. If that's the case, screw him. I mean, don't screw him. His loss.

I get this question a lot on HeTexted: "We went on a date two weeks ago. We text, but he hasn't asked me on a second date. Wassup with that?" I'd say he's being nice and doesn't want to dump you flat-out. What's he going to do? Say the honest but obnoxious thing, "We had fun but you're not my type"? Even a cold-hearted bastard would hesitate to send that. It doesn't mean you're not somebody's type. It just means this match didn't work out. He's replying to your texts out of politeness. If you stop, he will, too. Test it. See what happens.

There are some guys who will keep a text exchange going with a girl they're not into just because they like getting texts. It feels good to see an alert. That's it. It's like opening up a gift. Culturally, we're addicted to opening up gifts. I've texted girls for a month I never intended to pursue. They always replied, and I liked looking at my phone and having something to do instead of sitting there, staring into space. I'm addicted to the idea that someone wants to speak to me and is interested in what I have to say. Social validation comes via text message. Not the content—just the fact that you received a text. It's not just me, or bored, selfish pricks. I hear girls say, "I don't really like him, but I like getting texts."

Here's where I'll draw a dividing line between people under thirty and over thirty. The over-thirties might find texts from people they don't care about to be a nuisance. The under-thirty crowd? We'd rather hear from people we don't care about than hear from nobody. If you don't get alerts, notifications, and e-mails for a few hours, it's like you don't exist. A silent phone? It's a new, disturbing kind of quiet. When that quiet happens, you feel like you have to get something going right away. You look at Facebook. You look at Twitter. You look at e-mail. You do a lap. If you've got nothing happening, then, yeah, you might text the girl you don't like just to make noise, just to have something to do.

want

Signs You Have Good Textual Chemistry

* The banter is lively. His texts make you smile and laugh.

* The pace is brisk. The back-and-forth text volley is as blistering as a Serena Williams match.

* A funny reply is always at the tips of your fingers.

* The tone is light. He's killing himself to sound casual so you don't freak out and thinks he's *too* into you.

* The texts have a purpose, namely, making plans for your next date.

do not want

Signs You Have Bad Textual Chemistry

* He goes overboard with flattery. Not to say you aren't the most beautiful woman within a three-hundred-mile radius of Chicago, but gushing by text is the hallmark of a Player.

* His texts often begin, "Waiting for the bus." That's not a flirty text; it's a cry for help—helping him kill time when he's bored. No need to answer that call.

* The banter is deadly. His texts make you frown and groan.

* You're out of tune. You can't tell if he's being ironic; you find yourself wondering, "What'd he mean by that?" "Is he for real?" and "I don't get it."

(65)

✻ You're out of sync. You reply within minutes; he replies within days.

✻ You're stalled. You text back and forth forever, but he never asks you out. He's just using you to keep his thumbs limber.

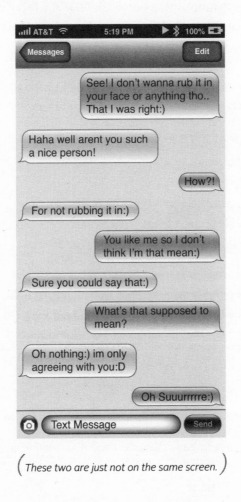

(These two are just not on the same screen.)

autocorrect

If you find yourself typing, "What's going on?" or "What's up?" please stop. Variations of "Wassup?" are the spam of text: easy to ignore, a pain in the ass, and generally bogus and annoying. You might as well write, "I've got nothing to say, but I'm inflicting myself on you anyway while trying to come off as nonchalant. Haha."

the memo

✳ **Rule of Thumb(s):** There is an inverse relationship between a guy's text tone and his interest in you. If he's effusive in his praise, he's not all that into you. If he's ironic and subtle, he's way into you. An aggressive, intense tone means he couldn't care less. He keeps it light? Then he cares.

✳ Texting limbo is when you go back and forth for over a month without him asking you out. It's the worst kind of romantic purgatory. Put an end to it by texting, "Would love to set something up. Let me know." If he doesn't fall on that like a ton of bricks, he's either chickenshit or not into you.

(4)

you texted . . . again

You are woman! You can text! It's 2014
(last time we checked). Women initiate
hostile bank takeovers. We run for
president. We can send the first text.
And the second. And the third . . . right?

the context

You're a strong and powerful (not to mention gorgeous and brilliant) woman, absolutely. And you have every right to text a guy. Hey, the COO of Facebook herself wrote a whole book called *Lean In*, telling women not to be passive and all lady-like. She'd probably urge women to lean into their relationships as well. Send that text! Be unafraid! And if the first text goes unanswered, don't cower and say, "He's not into me." Go for what you want. Hammer away. Eventually, you'll break through the glass ceiling and his wall of silence.

Hey it's ▓▓▓ I got your number from ▓▓▓

Oh hey. Whats up

It was great meeting you, I had fun last night

Word. Me too

How about drinks sometime?

Sounds like a plan

Have you ever been to the hub?

Whats that

the subtext

(B-E aggressive!
Be be aggressive!)

carrie

Initiating text. It's a risk, and risk is rewarded in life. But it's not female empowerment that leads women to send a double or triple text. It's paranoia. Haven't heard back from a text in over twenty-four hours? Your head starts to spin the scenarios, and the only thing that'll stop the downward wacka-doo spiral is a reply text. Maybe he forgot to reply. What's a little harmless "Did you see my text?" text?

Well, it's not so harmless if you genuinely like the guy. Twenty-four hours is nothing. Maybe he's (actually) busy at work. Maybe he doesn't feel like being in touch today. Sure as hell, if you keep sending him texts and acting like a needy, insecure, possessive girl-friend by texting multiple times, he'll never reply. Think about it: When a friend does that to you, don't you find it annoying? Stop texting him and give him a little breathing room. Everyone needs space sometimes with-out feeling like they're being bombarded by a nutbag who's throwing nuts from her bag. The truth hurts. Sorry about that.

My husband told me once that he was see-ing this girl for a few months, but he had to end it because of a single texting incident. After I gleefully asked for more details (why do we take such sick pleasure in hearing about the crazy girls who came before?), Matt said, "She called me four times in a matter of thirty minutes, then followed up with seven— *seven*—rapid-fire texts asking, 'Where r u?' and 'Where the F R U?'" He was at his office working, but he didn't want to let on or she might storm lobby security.

An extreme example? You should see (you *will* see) what comes into HeTexted along this vein. I can see how it might've happened. When she didn't hear from him, the movie in her head started playing. It was starring Matt and a woman who wasn't her. Maybe her most bitter rival from high school? *Definitely* her most bitter rival from high school. Her jealousy erupted via text.

We've all done the double text, double e-mail, double Gchat. A double could come off as eager but forgivable. A triple text? That equals "stalker" to most guys. Even if your texts are calm, like, "Hey, what's up?" Followed an hour later with, "You must be busy." And then in another hour, "Make that *really* busy." He won't appreciate your restraint. It doesn't matter what you write. The only thing he cares about are those three pings, the three text bubbles in a row. He is definitely really, *really* busy—being annoyed by you.

His phone is in his hand. If he doesn't respond to the first text, the second one isn't going to make your case look better. When the third one comes in and goes unanswered, he feels like an asshole and blames you for it.

The phone isn't in his hand? Then how pathetic does it look later when he checks his messages and sees all those shout-outs from you? Kind of pathetic. "

The triple text: Shameful by any other name . . .

lisa

When you initiate a text conversation with a guy and he doesn't respond, you feel crushed. It's like being set adrift at sea. You've been ignored, made to feel unimportant and invisible, like you're nothing. You put your-

(73)

self out there on a limb and got nothing back, not even a "thanks for trying." That feeling creates a void that needs to be filled—ASAP. The quickest things to stuff in there are excuses. He's crazy busy. He's in a meeting. He's thinking of the exact right reply to send, and that takes time. He's in flight. His phone is dead. His phone is lost. He's lost. He's been in an accident. He's in a coma. He's dead.

The most bitter irony of it: Not getting any response makes you like the other person more. (When you thought he was dead in a ditch, you were devastated!) You become obsessed with him, and with the reason for his silence. You might do a stalker lap around his Facebook and Twitter, see if he updated during the span of your neglected texts. You can't let the phone out of your sight. Not that you'd reply immediately if he did deign to text (he made you wait for days; he can surely wait a few hours). But knowing he did reply, even with a few words, would take the anvils off your shoulders.

There are times when we can't control our inner creep, when we just throw in the towel on self-respect and send multiple texts. It is possible to transcend crazy and sail right into comedy or a new form of performance art (performance texting?). I've done this, and I couldn't stop texting and laughing at how horrible it was at the same time. That's when you really need to lock your phone in a drawer and go to a party, or out with friends. "

so he's into me . . .
even if i initiate every exchange and send a few follow-ups if need be?

Bro Consensus: With all due love and respect for all womankind, *HELL NO!*

brian

It's okay for you to initiate texting. If he's wondering about mutual interest, he'll be relieved when she makes contact. If you send the text in the right way—not looking desperate or too eager—great. You can be the aggressor and still come across as sweet and nice. Something along the lines of, "Hey, it was cool to hang out with you. Hope to see you around," could work. A wavering guy will gain enough confidence in your interest to step up and take it from there.

A guy who stops texting altogether? The writing is on the phone screen—by its not being there. If it's been a few hours, then he's just busy. But if he doesn't reply to you for

(75)

several days, it means he's lost interest. Or he's dead in a ditch. "

(Down, girl!)

kenny

In this one area, just this one area, guys need to feel like they're calling the shots. After we got married, my wife knew she was calling the shots and we're okay with that. But in the beginning, a guy likes to make first contact. He wants to send the first text and ask you out first. And then, he wants to follow up first.

Sure, women can initiate, and it could be okay. If he already likes you, he might be flattered. But if he's not into you, it won't matter.

You can't text a guy into you.

You are not one witty message away from true love.

He can't be won over by your determined effort. I do think that a man can wear a woman down with hot pursuit. But a guy doesn't care what you text, no matter how clever, if he's not attracted. He'll want to be friends. He might take the sex, but he won't want a relationship.

Why? A lot of attraction is how you make him feel. He wants to feel like the hunter, not the hunted. It was true before the first cell phone. Before the telephone. Before the telegraph. It'll be true no matter what technology is available. Now, some men will respond to your texts with an LOL. Unless he's pushing the exchange forward—asking questions, asking you out—he's just being polite.

And if he stops replying, it's not the kiss of death. It depends how long it's been. If it's one or two days, he's having a bad day or taking time off to sit around and do nothing, or hanging with the guys. Some of us need to recharge on romance, too, on occasion. Taking a break gives us a chance to miss you and feel excited about talking, texting, or seeing you again soon. (FYI: According to Guy Time, "soon" is within a week. According to Girl Time, "soon" is apparently within the hour. I was married for a couple years before I figured that out.) Don't flip out when he has an off-text day. Just be patient and see if things turn around tomorrow. If his off-text days are greater than his on-text days, though, you might have something to worry about. **"**

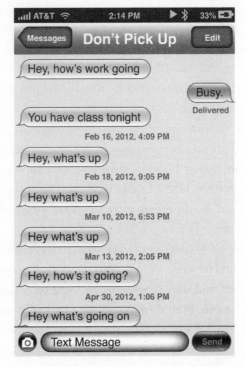

The sextuple text: Self-humiliation over a two and a half months' span???

.ıll AT&T 🛜   2:14 PM   ▶ ⁎ 33% 🔋

Messages **Don't Pick Up** Edit

Hey, how's work going

Busy.
Delivered

You have class tonight

Feb 16, 2012, 4:09 PM

Hey, what's up

Feb 18, 2012, 9:05 PM

Hey what's up

Mar 10, 2012, 6:53 PM

Hey what's up

Mar 13, 2012, 2:05 PM

Hey, how's it going?

Apr 30, 2012, 1:06 PM

Hey what's going on

Text Message   Send

brian

If he doesn't pick up what you threw down, don't send another text! Sending multiple texts that go unanswered is a Very. Bad. Idea. I sure as hell wouldn't send another if that happened to me! I'm not a glutton for rejection. I can take the hint that no response means she's not into me. Most women get the message loud and clear, too. To the women out there who don't, let me spell it out: If he likes you, he will reply. If he wants you, he will initiate. If he doesn't, he won't. If you double text him, he'll be doubly inclined to ignore you. Triple text? Turned off times ten. It grows exponentially. There should be some kind of metric for it.

Multiple texts are a sign of desperation. I'm sure there are guys out there who would be happy to find a desperate woman—but not the kind of dude that a self-respecting girl would throw away her dignity to pursue.

If you're in an established relationship and he won't reply to texts, I'd say he's pissed off and doesn't want to go there on a tiny screen. Even then, no matter how badly you want an explanation, just let it go. Step away from the iPhone. Leaving things open is a better move. I'm probably going to sound a little chauvinistic saying this, but several of my other girlfriends have said how much women love drama. I think a lot of over-texting is that urge for drama. "I sent him five texts and he didn't reply!" makes a better agony story than just letting it go and moving on. Most guys would just rather not deal. They can easily detach themselves from drama and any situation that might turn into a headache. Girls want an answer, even if it's a rejection. Guys will think a non-response *is* an answer. If a woman keeps sending texts, he'll just ignore them and do something else.

jared

I don't fault you for wanting to text first. It's a nice thing, but only if she's got something to say. Quick story: I'm a comedian, and I go to Foxwoods, a casino in Connecticut, to perform a lot. There's this girl who comes to the shows. We met backstage and hooked up once. She still texts me once a week to say, "What's up?" I never answer unless she asks about my next show at Foxwoods. I write to her then, not because I like her. I *do* like to have people in the audience, and she has a lot of friends. If she texts me days after the show—the "Hey, hon" treatment—I just ignore it. The texts I hate the most are when she writes, "Yo" or "Hey." She's just bored and looking for something to do. I've got nothing to say to her. Even if I ignore five texts in a row, she keeps coming at me with nonstarters. I think she's a little lonely. She's a nice person. I just don't want to take that on.

Don't text just to text. If he has something to say, he will. That's how a good relationship and conversation start. Call and response. No response? Then stop calling! If he's not answering you after the third text, you have to be done with it. Treat texting like a conversation. If you went up to a guy at a party and said three things to his face and he ignored you and acted like you hadn't spoken at all, you'd say, "What a dick!" and leave. Well, do the same thing if he ignores three texts in a row.

Ask yourself, Why are you texting him? To get to know more about his life? You're not going to succeed on the freakin' phone. But if you text to go on a date soon, when you're together, you might learn whether you really like him or not. 99

Huh, you just confused the hell out of me.

AND now it seems like you're mad. We just don't talk as friends like we did oh, 3 weeks ago? In my opinion maybe I'm wrong.

You seriously aren't making much sense. You're reading into things too much. We've in the past three weeks gone to a movie, talked on the phone, and text occasionally. It's the end of the year and we're all very busy.

Kind of hate the dude for calling her out on crazy, but he might be right.

want

Honestly, we're stumped to come up with a clear case of Want for a guy who blatantly ignores text after text. Unless . . . you happen to be a masochist and can only feel true joy and satisfaction when emotionally tormented by a shithead. Then, okay. Fine. A sadistic text withholder is the perfect guy for you. Mazel tov! You're a match. For you non-masochists, a relationship is a dialogue. If only one person is staying in touch or pushing things forward (or backward or sideways), that's not a relationship. It's a delusion.

do not want

* Belittling, mocking rejecters.

HE TEXTED ME THIS...

Oct. 16, 2012, 2:18 PM

> Sooo...was that a wink in the hallway today??

> Was it?

> Soo.... was it?

Who is this?

> You know who! I sit behind you in English.

This phone is no longer in service

...SO NOW I'M WONDERING?

I had texted this guy pretty regularly a couple months ago and then we didn't for a while. Then, yesterday he looked super hot so I sent this to him but I don't no why he doesn't want to talk to me?!

(*Cringe. Can we all agree that high school SUCKS!?*)

This poor girl doesn't seem to understand the basic principles of talking to boys. Do not put them on the spot, and never assume a boy winks non-mockingly or unironically.

(83)

She's clueless and sweetly but tragically genuine. On the other hand, he's a douchebag with training wheels. Not too many ways to make "stop texting me" any clearer than this. When you get a text from a guy who literally says, "Stop texting me," or, "I'm deleting your number," he's not JKing. He means it. We hope this kid gets his heart broken *to bits* in college.

Some men freak out when backed into a corner, in a bar or text window. If he can't extricate himself kindly and compassionately, he is not a gentleman. He is not worthy of your kiss emojis, or your longing looks at the back of his softly curling hair in English class. Don't be a chump, patsy! If you have a shred of dignity, half a shred, do yourself a favor and move to another desk.

❋ Cursing sons of bitches

(Who you calling Bitch, Bitch??)

❋ Your demands to know where he is and what he's doing are not an electronic truth serum. A guy won't buckle under the pressure, confess or apologize. He'll just ignore the texts. If he does reply and comes back at you with hostility—like this tool—he's not worth it.

❋ Sending repeat texts can give us insight into ourselves. In this case, the woman's texts show her how little faith and trust she has in this guy. Fortunately, an exchange like this can also reveal the guy's true nature. Is he a trustworthy mensch or a complete scumbag whom you should never see or contact again? We were appalled by this exchange. As an adjective, i.e., *bitchy*? We can see it. But "bitch," used as if it were your proper name? Heck no. Not okay. Don't take "bitch" from anyone, except your best friends.

❋ Obviously, when we feel vulnerable and insecure, we might text too much and likely live to regret it. But in this case, it was worth it. She might never learn where he really was. But she did learn that he's a grade-A asshole. When a man calls you a bitch—in text or in person—your relationship has respect issues. No matter how annoying a woman is by double or triple texting, he shouldn't go over the line. He might as well have texted, "Never contact me again." That's how much he cares. For a peek at his true nature, the insult might be worth the insight.

autocorrect

∗ "What's up?" ⟶ "How'd your thing go on Thursday?"

∗ "Haven't heard from you in a while. Did you lose your phone?" ⟶ "Hey! I lost my phone. If you haven't heard from me for a while, that's why."

∗ "Where the hell ARE YOU?" ⟶ "If you don't reply in the next ten minutes, you are slime covered in mucus with a dusting of leprosy. SUCK IT!!!"

Don't really send that last one. Remember when you were a kid and got furiously mad at your bestie? Your mom told you to write your feelings in a letter, to scribble all your vicious takedowns and bitter accusations on the page. Get it all out, put it all down, and then, said wise Mom, "Never send it." You downloaded the anger, and now you feel better and are back in emotional control.

You can write Never Send Texts to douches, too—but only on actual paper with an actual pen. It's a lot easier to stop yourself from addressing and stamping an envelope, than from hitting the Send or envelope-icon button.

the memo

✳ Go ahead and send the first text. But stop there. If he doesn't reply and one-up your bravery by asking you out, he's either (1) rude, (2) stupid, (3) not into you, or (4) all of the above.

✳ If you don't get a response to two texts in a row, you have to stop. If you keep at it, you'll come off as crazypants.

✳ Your texts should have a purpose. Ask a relevant question, something only he can answer. Send him a link that pertains to something he's into. If you haven't spoken in a month, then what could you be "checking in" about? To remind him, in case he forgot, that you exist and would very much like to touch his penis? He might take you up on the sex, but don't hold your breath for a relationship.

✳ Only send a string of angry texts if you're in a serious relationship. Otherwise, you will get completely blown off. It's a lot more fun to fight in person, anyway. Save your best lines for face-to-face arguments.

✳ If you find yourself being double or tripled texted, and (therefore) aren't interested in him romantically, how to let the guy down easy? You can take a screen from a guy's textbook and just ignore, ignore, ignore. Or, you can take a kinder, gentler approach, and say, "I'm getting the feeling from how often you text that you might like me a little. I thought you should know, I'm seeing someone else right now." You don't have to tell the absolute truth, that the person you're "seeing right now" happens to be the old lady at the dry cleaner's. He will get the point: not available/interested/otherwise inclined to entertain his many texts.

are you a stalker?

This girl has definitely gone off the deep end . . .

HE TEXTED ME THIS...

Oct. 17, 2012, 3:19 PM

So. Did you like my outfit today? I picked it especially for you.

Didn't you get that last text?

Oh I didn't really notice. sorry :/

Well, I'm still wearing it. And I'm outside your house! Let me in!

...SO NOW I'M WONDERING?

I'm pretty sure this guy likes me. We've talked before and I drive by his house almost every night. I drive by at like two miles an hour so he'll notice me but I don't think that he does. He didn't even let me in that one night! But I know we're perfect for each other and we're gonna get married. Should I give him some space for our love to grow?

Have you, too? Signs you're a . . .

One-Alarm Stalker

✻ You check his Wall once a day.

✻ You follow his Twitter feed in stealth mode.

✻ You occasionally Google him.

Two-Alarm Stalker

✻ You read his feeds and Google him more than twice a day.

✻ You track him on Foursquare.

✻ You investigate his female Facebook Friends and compare yourself to them favorably, as in, "I'm so much hotter than her! What's he doing commenting on her link to that stupid meme?"

Three-Alarm Stalker

✻ You do a stalker lap of his social media feeds more than three times a day.

✻ You get his work address from LinkedIn and use Google maps to see how long it would take you to get there and back by car, via public transportation, and on foot.

✻ You use people-search sites to get his home address and actually pay $9.95 for the info. You research routes to his place from your home and office, in various outfits—casual, business, evening, ninja.

(89)

Four-Alarm Stalker

✳ You drive by his house at 5 mph hoping he'll see you.

✳ You park on his block with a sandwich, a cup of coffee, and an empty two-liter bottle to pee in.

✳ You bang on his door at 3 A.M., screaming, "Let me in!"

✳ You are dragged away from his house in handcuffs.

✳ He takes out a restraining order.

Five-Alarm Stalker

✳ You ignore the restraining order.

✳ You make a bunch of dolls that play a recording of your voice saying, "I love you" and hide them throughout his house.

✳ You erect a shrine in your basement consisting of pictures of him, samples of his hair, and things he's touched at some point.

✳ You lure him to your basement so he can appreciate the shrine . . . and who knows what'll happen? Hope he's into chains! Color you fifty shades of :))))))

(5)

he group texted

The guy likes threesomes and foursomes
and orgy-like tensomes—digitally
speaking. When he texts you, you're just
one name on a list. He has a predilection
for mass e-mails. Or he always asks
about other people in his notes.

the context

You might have heard the expression, "When you get in bed
with a guy, seven other people are in there with you." The
idea is that all your experiences and hang-ups and childhood
weirdness and religious influences, etc. are present in your
mind when you are at your most self-conscious, defense-
less and excited. It's not that, literally, that your mother and
priest and the ex-boyfriend who once described your thighs
as "thick" are actually in bed with you. But you are thinking
about them, if subconsciously.

Nowadays, we can amend that old saying to, "When you text on your phone, 1,238 other people are on-screen with you." Any text or e-mail has the potential to be forwarded to your Facebook friends or copied into an e-mail. Put aside the entire privacy nightmare of how easy it is to share ANYTHING electronically. The issue that comes up a lot on HeTexted is when a guy only seems to contact a girl as part of a group (for example, he asks her to join a Facebook event, or adds her info to one of his text lists). A similar situation is a guy always mentioning other people in his private messages to her, like tagging friends without the photo, as in, "How's it going? I was out last night with Jon and Bill and Harry at O'Malley's. Drunk times . . . Do you know those guys?" When they connected digitally, they were never really alone.

It's personal but impersonal. It's direct but indirect. It's satisfying to see his name pop up on your notification and text alerts. But then you realize he's talking to a dozen other people in addition to you.

the subtext

carrie
Women are excellent at rationalizing any male behavior. You might think, *So what if he only e-mails me in a group? He takes strength in numbers. He's shy and insecure*

*about reaching out to just me. He needed all
those other people as a buffer.*

The Shy Guy is a straw man, ladies! He
doesn't exist. Yes, we have seen the Shy Guy
in every teen movie ever made. He's charming
and befuddled and insecure whenever he gets
close enough to a real-life female to smell her
honeysuckle shampoo. Guess what? Men who
are genuinely, paralytically shy are so crippled
by their anxieties, you will not find them
charming and adorable. You won't even notice
them, and certainly wouldn't find them worthy of your obsession. If you are attracted to a
guy, it's likely other women have found him
attractive too. The Shy Guy has probably gotten laid a thousand times because women are
seduced by his vulnerable, bashful humility.

The group texter is a great example of a
guy who can't commit to a girl enough to
send her a solo message. That's the opposite
of shy! He's not using the mass e-mail as a
buffer. It's more like a shield, fending off the
hope of any of the women on his list who
may feel they are special to him.

lisa

An invitation is an invitation
is an invitation. He is expressing *some* desire to see you. If he

didn't want you to go to the party, he wouldn't have included you on his list. But he's not singling you out. Sending a group text or mass e-mail invite is not asking you on a date. What is a date? A private meeting where you will talk, just the two of you, look each other in the eye, and devote your attention to each other for an hour or more. Making the plans involves some thought and effort. A man in pursuit of a woman makes the effort. He puts time, thought, and energy into getting her alone.

But throwing your contact info onto his invite list takes next to zero effort. When a man expends zero energy to get you to go somewhere, you just can't read anything into it. Unless you are an established couple, a group invite doesn't scream, "He wants you." He wants a big turnout for his party, though. If you're unsure where you stand with him, being a face in the crowd won't clue you in.

But let's play devil's advocate. Say, of the fifty people on his list, you're the one he really hopes to see turn up at the bar. He might be nervous to single you out because he's (sigh) shy. By answering the cattle call, though, you give him permission to be a coward. Do you really want a guy who is *that* insecure? Even less confident guys, if they liked you, would try to make you feel special. Maybe the group text is a fishing expedition. It's his way to find out how you feel about him. He's going to have to try a little bit harder than that for such privileged information!

If it's open bar, by all means, go to the party. Bring your friends. Have a good time. Should the man in question talk to you there, that's lovely, well, and good. But if you're really into him, be friendly, but don't follow him around all night. Hold out for an invitation to drinks or dinner. You both deserve to go through the solo ask-out process. Allowing him to use group texts as a crutch is weak on both sides.

so he's into me . . .
if i'm on a group text list?

Bro consensus: He's as into you as he is into the other twenty-seven girls on the list.

brian

Whoa, Carrie and Lisa are taking a hard line on the group texter! My girlfriend and I started out group texting with a mutual friend. It was just the three of us, and then another friend joined in as well. So we had this four-way open, friendly communication. In our case—my girlfriend and I were both seeing other people at the time—we needed

(95)

a soft way of contacting each other. That way, if it didn't work out between us, we could say, "Nothing going on here. We've got witnesses." Ultimately, we got used to texting each other as part of a group, and that did make the transition to private exchanges smoother. It made things less awkward.

Any opportunity for people to connect and explore their feelings is good. You can see how someone handles him or herself in a group situation, how they related to the others, which is important to know. You get to establish a context and some textual chemistry. But after a time, you have to put down the group-text crutch. It's an introduction. After a few days to a few weeks, you need to be in direct, one-on-one contact. Oh, and the person who makes first non-group contact? It should be the guy.

> It was cool hanging out
>
> Yea if you're out tonight, bring ▬? We're going to ▬▬▬
>
> Awesome will tell her! Can't wait to see you
>
> Ok

He asks to see your hot friend in a text? Not a good sign.

jared

I would *never* want to be on a group text with a girl I just started dating. You have no control over what the other people might say. If it's me, two of my friends, and the girl, I guarantee you one of my friends will text something that will embarrass me or her or everyone. Group texting is a virtual hangout. It's like watching a football game in someone's living room. Things get said. Jokes get made. A friend might make a totally offensive comment about an ex of mine. It's just too risky. I wouldn't allow a girl I liked to be exposed to ten seconds of that. Not that I have so much to hide. I have a little to hide. But the context would be completely wrong, and not romantic. Bringing a girl into a group text with my friends would be like bringing a new date to a frat basement or to a tailgate party. I'd feel uncomfortably responsible for her and worried what might happen. I can't imagine being okay with that situation with a girl for . . . ever? I really can't say. I haven't gotten that far yet. My relationships tend to end around the one-year mark. I'm sure that means something.

I have no idea why any woman would want to be involved. Why would that be at all fun for her? She might appreciate a glimpse inside my friendships. But she'll more likely be horrified and disgusted.

A text to twenty people that says, "I'm having a party tonight, come by," is what I call a soft invite. You and this guy just met. He's feeling it out, trying to see if you even remember who he is. In this situation, it's okay to text back privately to follow up. Something casual like, "So what's this party?" It's how you can feel him out after he sent you the soft invite to feel you out. Depending on his reply, you'll figure out if he's just trying to fill a room, or wants to see you in particular. Or, even better, just don't join the Facebook event or RSVP at all to the group invite. If I really liked a girl, her non-response would put me on edge enough to send her a personal message that said, "Did you see that invite? I hope you can make it."

kenny

Shyness in men is a thing. Insecurity does happen.

If he group texts to invite you out with his friends, it's a great sign. He's looking for a stamp of approval from his boys. Including you in a group of men and women, I'd say he's got mixed interest. He's checking out how you relate to his crew.

He also wants to see if you give a shit about him. But it just doesn't have the same impact when he involves other people. Regardless of whether he's into you, I'm just not into his pulling this move in general. "

He asks to see your hot brother in a text? Sweetie, we hate to break it to you, but he's gay. Not your brother! (Or maybe he is, how do we know?) This dude plays for the other team.

want

A guy who loops you into a group text situation might need the buffer of mutual friends to kick off your conversation. If he's part of a very tight circle of friends, this might be their peculiar vetting process (which, theoretically, you Do Not Want; among friends, there's close, and then there's stranglehold). It's sort of cute that he wants to see if you like his pals and vice versa. But a group text—like group sex—feels embarrassing and awkward about five seconds after it's over. It rarely turns out to be as fun as you hoped it would.

However or whyever the group texting thing got started, it must stop within a week. This is a habit you must break. Kick that crutch out from under him. If he stumbles and falls without the support . . .

do not want

A relationship is between a man and a woman, a woman and a woman, a man and a man, or a man and a very special sheep named Gladys. It is NOT between you and forty-eight of his Facebook cronies. As long as you're a name on his list, it's not a relationship. Even if you're number one on his list, it's not a relationship. It's casual. It's a friendship. It's a hookup. For a relationship to qualify as romantic, and potentially permanent, there must be no list. There must be only YOU.

autocorrect

As soon as you realize he texted you as part of a group, introduce yourself. Be friendly. At the first opening, say, "Nice meeting you all. GTG." To the guy, say directly, "Steve, I'll talk to you later. Bye." Use his name. Then sign off. Hey, you're a busy woman. You can't hang out on a group text all day. You left the door open for him to pick up the conversation later. Ideally, he'll get the hint that your desire to chat again doesn't include the entire crew.

the memo

* A mass-e-mailed "soft invite" should be as appealing to you as a soft . . . hot dog. It's limp and mushy and nothing to get excited about.

* Only accept a group text to a *huge* party. It could be a blast, especially if the booze is flowing freely. But don't expect anything special from the host. Go with friends. Go with an open mind. But make no mistake: This is not a date. It's not even close to a date.

* He could invite you to a thousand parties and events. But unless he sends you a private message to meet up, just the two of you, it is not a date. If a date is what you really want, hold out for it.

(6)

he updated

We get so many WTF questions on HeTexted about a dude's Facebook Wall. You asked for it, you got it. Without further ado, we present . . .

the ultimate facebook wall decoder

Looking at his Wall is like being invited into his cyber home. One look around and you might be reminded of a frat basement, a castle, or an abandoned rusty shanty that will give you tetanus; a log cabin or a McMansion. Ideally, a guy's Wall will seem like a warm, homey place that you can see yourself fitting into quite nicely.

Women are right to examine his Wall as closely as the Rosetta Stone—or the Sorcerer's Stone. Everything you need to know about a guy is right there on it. It provides info about who he is as a dude and a human being, as long as you know how to interpret the clues.

For instance, what can you learn about a guy based on his . . .

profile picture

First things first: the photo itself. Yes, you want to see a picture that shows the man's actual face and body. If he's a bit cheeky and posts a profile picture of Lord Voldemort, Elvis, an astronaut, a cell of the Ebola virus or Bugs Bunny, okay. Funny (meh). People like being unconventional with their profile pictures because humor, irony. But it does beg the question, Is he hiding behind his big clip-art portfolio of jokes? Is his actual face too scary to post?

The profile picture itself isn't as revealing of his character as how often he changes it. If he updates it once a week, we'd call that self-indulgent. If he changes it more than twice a week, we call that obsessive and narcissistic. Facebook brings out the narcissist in all of us, to some extent. But a guy who fixates on his own profile pictures has fallen into the mythological pond where Narcissus stared at his own reflection (way before selfies) and drowned. You just know a rapid picture cycler never reads his news feed. He doesn't care what others are up to, only in how his Friends "like" his new pix. Count how many different profile pictures he's used in the last month. Divide it in half. If that number is higher than five, he's already madly in love—with himself.

handle

If his Facebook handle is different than his real name, you have to wonder why. Is he obscuring his name so his high school friends can't track him down and harass him about reunions? If so, smart man! He might use a nom du Facebook so his boss and colleagues can't find him, which is also totally acceptable. But consider the handle itself. Also, any use of the word *hound* is a bad sign, even in reference to dogs. If he puts "hound" together with any slang for female delicate parts, just ugh, ick, and blecch. He is a pig, even if he links ten times a day to childhood-disease-prevention websites.

info

His wacky sense of humor inspired him to list Reykjavík, Iceland, as his hometown. We let men enjoy themselves in this harmless way. Why not? He finds it amusing to say he's currently employed by Doctor Who. Very cute and what-ever. You have to be the judge of what your tolerance is for high-lariousness. When you're into the guy, it'll probably be sky-high. If he says he's currently employed by the Galactic Alliance, that his hometown is Tatooine, and that he went to college at Death Star, accept that you're crushing on a fanboy and just go with it. Anything that strikes you as funny-strange, or funny-psycho, as opposed to trying-to-be-funny-haha, should raise a red flag.

status updates

Obviously, if he updates regularly about crushing beer cans on his forehead or that he fantasizes about killing his boss/mother, you might want to back away slowly from the Wall. You are the only one who can judge your update tolerance for reading about how much fun he's having out with his buds and his brews. Like the guy who is a rapid updater of his profile picture, a man who relentlessly posts about his current location and activity seems a little self-obsessed. Special warning if he always seems to be in bars or strip clubs. Double special warning if his updates are of a theme, like, "Last night: Did I really puke the whole thing?" So check for timing. A guy who updates mid-event is the type who will check his messages mid-date. Uncool.

relationship status

Girls will say they're "In a relationship" with their best friend, "Married" to a Ryan Gosling, or "It's complicated" with J.Crew. But when they're actually in a relationship, engaged or committed to a real man, they take that shit seriously. A guy, though, doesn't care about this status, even when he should. A lot of HeTexted readers complain that their boyfriend is still "Single" way past the point of "In a relationship." The guy's standard response is, "I know where we stand. I don't need to tell the world." It's a major cop-out. But if it means so much to him, you can always be "In an open relationship" with him and his status.

A word on changing relationship status: A friend of ours recently got separated. She sent a mass e-mail to her friends announcing the split, and saying she had wanted to let us all know before she changed her status on Facebook. She didn't want anyone to see the update and be shocked or confused. We felt this was a thoughtful way to handle a sad situation. Another friend saw her ex had changed his status to "Engaged." They'd broken up only a couple of months before. She was floored by it and called him. He said, "I didn't tell you because I thought you'd be upset." Man, was she. She still is! For major changes, it's polite and compassionate to alert certain people beforehand—just the people close to the situation who deserve and need to know. Not the entire world. That's what Facebook is for.

tags

Does he repeatedly tag "friends who like bestiality?" That's a major Do Not Want in our book. Check for his repeatedly tagging an attractive woman other than you, or an attractive man who wears a T-shirt with a rainbow and unicorn on it.

comments

Go ahead and judge a man by his friends' comments. Just read them with a grain of salt. People try to be witty but wind up douchey.

photos

Baby pictures might be cute, but it could mean he peaked at age two. Is he always holding a beer can with his arms around four bimbos? If so, he's using pix to validate his coolness—the opposite of actual coolness. Any image that is supposed to telegraph the idea of "I'm in the right place and you're not" is also irritating. We have pet peeves about shots from chairlifts or snowy peaks. Guys need to prove that they've made it to the top—even if it's the top of a mountain they sat in a gondola to reach. It's fine to take a picture of the majesty of nature. But then to immediately tweet it with #masteroftheuniverse, #yetipatrol, or #hightimes? Kind of destroys the moment.

he's rosetta-stoning your wall, too

Does the glimpse into your metaphorical home evoke a Barbie Dream House or a lunatic asylum? Just like you, guys are searching for clues about who you really are as a person on Facebook. Under no circumstances should a woman make wholesale changes to her content in order to impress men. Your Wall represents who you are, and making alterations would be a deception. The thing about obfuscation to misrepresent yourself: The truth will eventually come out. Better that he make an accurate Wall assessment than that you date for three months before you realize that you were incompatible from day one.

Yes, knowledge is power. With power comes great responsibility. Another great responsibility? That's, like, the last thing you need with everything else on your plate. So be knowledgeable about what your Wall says about you. Be a powerful woman, and confident in your choices. But, we repeat, do NOT freak out and do a major Wall scrubbing. Well, maybe delete that one photo of you wasted at Casa Loco. Not your finest hour.

We asked **Jared** to give us his take on a girl's Facebook page. His report from the Wall:

jared's likes

** **A wide range of photos.** I want to know what she looks like dressed up, on the beach, hanging out, at a bar. I couldn't care less about the fashion but I appreciate a preview of what might show up at the restaurant on a date. Don't hate me for being honest. Women probably do the same thing (right?).

** **A lively interaction with her friends.** Guys want to see that she has some sort of life going on, and that her friends respond to her comments and "like" her updates. When a woman does all the "liking" and commenting and is ignored back, it makes me wonder. Do her own friends think she's a loser and blow her off?

** **Posts from old friends.** I scan to see if someone posted on her Wall, "Hey, haven't seen you in so long. How's it going?" That indicates to me that people from her past remember her and liked her enough to get back in touch. She didn't burn all her bridges. That's a good quality in a person.

jared's loathes

✻ **She posts a thousand times a day,** including on what she had for lunch. No one cares what anyone had for lunch! How many food pyramids do I need to see? NONE!! Same with beaches. Everyone is on vacation except for me.

✻ **She connects Twitter and Facebook.** To me, that means she's a social media addict. I want a girl who can put her phone down without panicking.

✻ **Her Wall is too self-promotional.** I'm the pot calling the kettle black on this one. If you read my Facebook wall, you'd think, *This guy's insane.* I put up videos of me annoying people in New York or raunchy bathroom humor sketches. I'm a comedian! I have to promote my shit. But if that's all you do, then it's like you don't have any real friends or real life away from work or your ego.

✻ **Her Wall is public.** She must be accessible to Friends only. A dangerous person shrugs off privacy settings. Not sexy-dangerous. Stupid dangerous. She must have missed the three million reports about identify theft and having your crap out there for anyone to see. No privacy means bad judgment.

✻ **She overshares.** You don't have to, say, post the video of your navel piercing or placenta birth to overshare. Nearly *any* personal stuff qualifies, as far as I'm concerned. Three profile pictures deep, if I see the girl and her ex-boyfriend kissing on New Year's Eve, it's more than I need to know. He looks like a decent guy. That's not the point. I like some mystery when

I date someone—I don't want to know if her exes are better looking than me. They looked so happy. What happened
there? These are third-date conversations, not pre–first date
assumptions. Technology makes dating move too quickly,
and that's to her detriment. She'll be more forgiving and willing to give a guy a chance, even if she doesn't like what she
sees on Facebook. A guy will just write her off and hang out
with his friends instead.

#imadouchebag

Some hashtags you never want to see him use unironically—
or ever, really.

#swag

#yolo

#epic

#thuglife

#jagerbomb

#winning

#brotips

#cantbelieveimstillsingle

#sunglassesatnight

#beerme

#herpes #surprise

#youreadouchebag

Some hashtags that will make him SO NOT into you.

#nofilter

#nomakeup

(111)

#bffls
#selfie
#artsy
#1D4Evah
#lovejunkie
#karmaisabitchandsoamI
#sexchange
#twerkinit
#mancandymonday
#pregnant #kidding

(7)

e txd

The guy only LOLs, WTFs, and OMGs. To
K or not to K? That is the ????

the context

You and the dude aren't strangers anymore. By now, you've
been on a few dates and are getting more comfortable with
each other. You notice that his texts are getting shorter. And
shorter. They're barely clearing half a line. He's taken to using
abbreves and responding to your questions with one- or two-
word replies. It comes off as rude, lazy—too comfortable.
You're not married yet! You're not juggling two careers and five
babies. No matter how busy he is, he can take thirty seconds
to send a decent text. After all, you send carefully worded,
spell-checked texts in grammatically correct complete sentences every time (well, some of the time). No matter what
you send, though, he replies with a not-so-special "K." When
he's feeling downright verbose, he goes for an "LMAO" or
"JK." Is the brevity of the reply or text any indication of the

depth of his feelings? Is it one of those upside-down Internet things, like how, if he flatters you, he doesn't care, but if he acts casual, he does? You need guidelines! What's a healthy ratio of words sent to words replied?

the subtext

lisa

Show of hands: Who actually falls on the floor laughing or cries out loud? And who among us has the power to laugh her ass off? If that were true, women wouldn't bother with yoga or running. They'd laugh their asses off the newfangled way: by abbreving. A guy who is LMAO and LOTFL, if he's to be taken literally, is not mentally stable. He might have a drug problem.

Seriously, abbreves have their place in texting. It's easier to type one letter or a few letters than a whole sentence. But do it too often, and it comes across as thoughtless. Abbreves transmit a message, but probably not the one you mean. If you don't care enough about the person to go the extra mile and type a complete sentence, then what kind of surprise birthday party are you going to throw? A really lame one, like having a few people gather at the neighborhood pub. No imagination. What kind of father is a chronic abbrever going to be? When he sits down to have "the talk" with your future son, he's definitely going to leave out all the details. Think about it. Abbreve abusers do not make good lovers.

Mmk, we don't think he's giving her guitar tips or anything else.

In digital dating, you have so little to go on in the first place. And then, when someone doesn't type out clear and cogent messages, you have next to nothing to build

(115)

on. Say you're in a restaurant, seated at the table with a date, and you ask, "How's your steak?"

He replies, "K."

And that pretty much is that. Where do you go from there? Abbreves are dismissive conversation killers. Texting should be like talking. You can take a few shortcuts, sure. But don't throw out 90 percent of the alphabet!

Personally, I find abbreves really annoying, but I don't necessarily attach romantic significance—or insignificance—to them. The key to seduction is ambiguity, right? For that reason alone, abbreves are intriguing. A Player might send the minimum number of syllables to keep you guessing about him. We ladies do like a mystery. The best kind of story is when you don't know what's going to happen next. A terse texter stirs up the imagination. The fewer words, the more you can read into them. We can connect the dots any way we want, create our own stories, and believe what we want to believe. Having that kind of power can be quite addictive. He only sends back a "K," after you just poured your heart out? You can run with that "K." You can massage it into any shape you like. His "K" might mean a hundred things. And that's just it. We have to play out all one hundred scenarios, until the next text comes in. Then we start all over again. "

carrie

You know how I feel about Shy. Even the shyest guys will work up the courage to put some thought into texting the girl they really like, especially when she's driving the bus forward. I don't know if anyone is *that* shy. The truth is probably that he just doesn't want to get stuck on the phone having a long exchange with you when he'd rather be doing . . . well, just about anything else. Staring into space. Reading on the toilet. Making a sandwich.

An alphabetically challenged texter might be a "man of few words." He speaks with his deeds and only talks when absolutely necessary. The type of guy didn't say a single word until he was nine years old, and then one night at dinner, he said, "Please pass the salt," because, until that moment, everything was okay. He just doesn't see the point of talking (or texting) for talking's (or texting's) sake. Some women need constant reassurance to feel secure in a relationship. If you are one of them, a short-worded texter is not the right man for you. You'll feel frustrated and perpetually on edge. Now, some women's reassurance needs are deeper than the pit of hell. A dude could type poetic texts to her until his thumbs were worn to the knuckle and she wouldn't be satisfied.

HE TEXTED ME THIS...

.atl AT&T 🔋   1:45 PM   ▶ ⚹ 70% 🔋

Messages   **Edit**

> Ok. Well, I would like to see you again: if you are up for it

Yea

> You are a very short-worded person.

I'm sorry :-(

> Its ok. Its intriguing. I just don't want to annoy you

No your not I'd let u know if you are

Read 1:44 PM

📷 (Text Message)   Send

...SO NOW I'M WONDERING?

We hooked up and now we are to this point. He takes a long time to reply to texts. And when he does, he is very short worded. Does he like me? Or, is he just shy? If he is short-worded, then, it is cute. But if he just doesnt want to talk to me, then, that is a problem.

Meta annoying? She's worried she's annoying an annoying abbrever.

so he's into me . . .
if he's a texter of few letters?

Bro consensus: WCSFSBPNSIYS*

brian

Abbreves are extremely stupid, like you're back in high school with your first real girlfriend, typing your secret code to each other. Frankly, when a girl texts me abbreves, she sounds like a ditz. It's the textual equivalent of baby talk. They might've made sense back in the day when you didn't have a keyboard on your phone, just a number pad, and you had to hit five buttons to get a single letter. But if you're over eighteen, it's immature to use "LOL." It's disingenuous. When people type "LOL," they're not laughing, they're mocking. If someone is really amused, they type "hahaha," which, although short, just seems more sincere. I guess that's the thing. Abbreves are post-ironic. They come off as meaningless and snide. Spelled-out words or phrases come off as genuine and real.

When a guy uses abbreves, you can't really dig a lot of meaning out of his texts, in terms of his romantic interest. But you can get

---

* We can't say for sure but probably not so into you. Sorry.

an idea of who he is. You could think, *He's cool*, or, *He's a pretentious idiot*. But you will never think, *He's a smart, thoughtful, considerate person who goes the extra mile*. No guy is going to be outright disrespectful and rude to a woman he is genuinely into. A dude of few letters might come off as shy. But I don't see what that has to do with typing half a word or a full sentence. I do believe a guy who takes a while to respond with a haiku of abbreves is not sending you a love poem. He isn't making an effort and/or he doesn't have

.ıll AT&T 📶   12:25 PM   ▶ ∗ 43% 🔋

‹ Messages   Edit

> hahaha

I think you're pretty 😔

> aww thanks 😊

But I have a girlfriend...

> yeah I know haha

Yeah

> haha what's that gotta like do with

Nothing haha, I was just saying it

> oh okay haha

📷 (Text Message   ) Send

Hahahaha: An abbreve for "Cheating is funny."

much to say. As I've said before, when a guy doesn't break a metaphorical sweat, he's not into you.

kenny

Lisa was right to say that one-word replies and abbreves do make a guy hard to read, and that leaves the door open for a girl to come up with theories to explain his mysterious text. Is he shy? Is he busy? Is he illiterate?

"Shy" and "busy" are the two biggest excuses girls make for bad male behavior. You should get in the habit of replacing "shy" with "rude," and "busy" with "neglectful" every time you rationalize his being a jerk. Instead of, "He probably wants to text me, but he's just shy," change it to, "He wants to text, but he's rude." Instead of, "I should have heard from him by now. He must be crazy busy," change to, "I should have heard from him. He must be really crazy neglectful—and a real idiot, too."

Regarding "haha," "JK," "LOL," "LMAO," "ETC," this is a man you can't trust. What if he texted, "You're a pain in the ass. Stop bothering me. Haha JK"? Too much JKing isn't funny. It's sadistic. But I can see how a girl would justify it by thinking, *He's got a weird sense of humor,* or, *Jokes don't translate over text.* Especially when they're not funny.

The effort he makes is an exact measure of his interest in you. If he uses hardly any words, he's hardly interested. If he uses abbreves, he's probably just being polite and is trying to send the message that this is all you'll get from him—by text, or anything else. A chronic JKer doesn't want you to take him seriously—by text, or anything else. Think how hard it would be to have a real-life conversation with a guy who only gave you yes or no answers. You'd know in five seconds that he wasn't into you. Same thing by text. If you leave all the work of keeping it going to the short-worded texter, he's probably not going to bother. Neither should you.

We have one word for the man of few words: Douchebag.

jared

Hold on, bros. I think guys are clueless about what a girl expects. I was dating a girl. It was her birthday and I texted, "Happy birthday." She got mad at me because there was no exclamation point.

I never would have thought to put "!!!!!!" at the end of "Happy birthday." It seemed enough to remember to send the greeting on the right day. But when I tell that story onstage, girls laugh right away. Guys just don't think of the subtle (or not-so-subtle) implications of every letter and punctuation mark in a text. We know about the importance of tone, though.

Guys can't live in this world where they don't know their relationships hang in the balance over an exclamation point. We don't really care about that stuff, but we have to. I don't assume a short-worded texter is shy or busy. He might just be a clueless schmo who has no idea what the girl needs and expects from him. He also might be a rude jerk. Does he keep making dates or not? If he does, then don't go nuclear over a missing "!!!".

Personally, I am not going to throw around exclamation points and LOLs. It's just not my style. But I can see how exclams make a difference. I just had this exchange yesterday:

Me: "Hey, you want to get together tonight?"

Her: "Yeah, sure"

Me: "You sound really excited"

Her: "Haha I totally am"

Very ambiguous. I have no idea if she even wants to see me. She might totally stand me up. Is the "yeah, sure" more of a "yeah, right"? Was the "I totally am" with an eye roll or for real? I'm definitely not asking for a wink or fifteen smiley faces. That'd be too cutesy, although I could stomach it from a girl I really like.

I cannot stand "LOL" from *anyone, anytime*, no matter how hot she is. It's bullshit! I will never send "LOL" to anyone, even if I were really laughing out loud. "LOL" is an L-I-E. It's like cheap filler, what you write when you have nothing to say. As I've made clear, if a girl has nothing to say, then SAY NOTHING. Some girls write "LOL" at the beginning and end of every text. I don't want to see that. I know you are totally fucking lying. If people laughed as much as they wrote "LOL," they would be clinically insane. I want genuine laughter. Overloading on "LOL" is a sign of dishonesty. What else will she exaggerate about? I don't want to know. Far preferable: "haha I'm smiling." A girl sent that to me once, and I smiled when I read it. It seemed sweet and genuine.

When you receive an "XO" from a girl, it's nice.

When you get an "XX," it's cute.

When you get an "XXX," it's poison or porn.

If a girl signed off with, like, a thousand "XOs" in a row, I would think she was crazy. Would you kiss someone like that in real life? That would feel like my grandmother grabbing my face and smooching me on parents' weekend at camp.

You want your words to have some power. When he abbreves, LOLs, or sends really short texts, he's giving up his power. The only reason someone would willfully squander power was if he didn't care about having it in the first place.

want

Signs You Have Good Textual Compatibility

✳ You type with your heart on your sleeve; he's just as articulate and out there.

✳ The ration of your words to his is no less than 1:2. Even

if you text more actual lines, he always replies to adequately answer your question or address your concern.

✳ Size doesn't matter as much as substance. You both agree that, short or long, a text deserves a sufficient reply.

do not want

Signs You Have Bad Textual Compatibility

✳ You're open and emotional; he's dismissive and practical.

❊ You're genuine and honest; he's JKing and "messin'" with you.

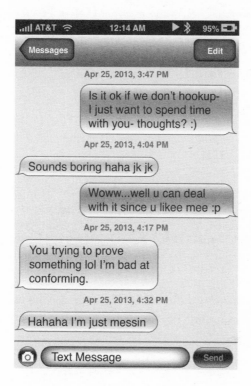

❊ Your texting ratio is higher than 1:2. Your texts are clear and thoughtful; his replies are terse and dismissive.

autocorrect

Women, you just have to spell it out for the guys. Say, "When you send short texts, it makes me feel disrespected. I would very much appreciate it if you could send better texts. Just chalk it up as one of the little things you do for me even if it seems stupid."

If he replies, "K," you can either LOL or FCOL. Your call.

Otherwise, if you keep sending him cogent texts and you get the equivalent of a grunt in reply, you need to go black-ops silent for a while. Wait and see what golden prose he texts next.

the memo

✻ Don't confuse short texts with shyness. He's not afraid to text you eloquently. He just doesn't feel like it.

✻ When he types "LOL," he's not laughing. He's mocking.

✻ When you type "LOL," he's gagging.

✻ If he JKs about the little things, one day, he might type, "Let's get married! JK!" To which you can reply, "I'm pregnant! JK!"

(8)

he ranted

He sent a text that might have been
a novel in progress, a political speech,
or an epic poem. Does the length and
passion of his text prove the depth of his
feelings for you?

the context

The long-winded texter (aka the short-worded texter's blo-
viating cousin) sent you another long diatribe about how
beautiful your hair looks in the sunlight or how the U.S.
Constitution need a page-one rewrite, or how Marvel kicks
mutant ass all over DC Comics any day of the week. He's not
afraid to leave a text trail a mile long, which says a lot about
his gumption—or complete lack of judgment.

You'd think, given the usual truncated condition of the
majority of men's texts, that receiving a long, passionate message from a man would be a relief. With so many words in
one bubble, his feelings should be exhaustingly clear. Even if

his missive isn't riddled with typos and unintelligible gibberish, you often can't tell what the hell he's talking about. Often, the longer the text, the cloudier the message. Forest, trees, etc. We find it particularly frustrating, when, after a three-screen-long text, he finishes up by asking himself, "What was I talking about?" Yeah. Exactly. He could have saved you both a lot of time by writing, "I'm drunk off my ass right now."

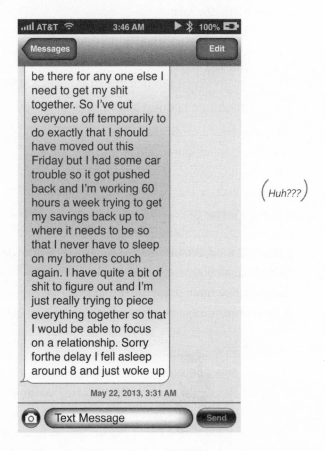

be there for any one else I need to get my shit together. So I've cut everyone off temporarily to do exactly that I should have moved out this Friday but I had some car trouble so it got pushed back and I'm working 60 hours a week trying to get my savings back up to where it needs to be so that I never have to sleep on my brothers couch again. I have quite a bit of shit to figure out and I'm just really trying to piece everything together so that I would be able to focus on a relationship. Sorry forthe delay I fell asleep around 8 and just woke up

(Huh???)

May 22, 2013, 3:31 AM

the subtext

carrie

I'm going to make this really short, and spare readers in a relationship with a Ranter the eyestrain: The man of many words is 90 percent full of crap. Gushing is for geysers, not guys. You become wordy when actions can't speak for you. If he's complaining, exaggerating, and making excuses via text, he's trying to make up in words for bad behavior. Or he's overcompensating with words for lack of genuine emotion. If you can't put up, then you type up.

Not in all cases. I'm sure some long-winded texters are honest, upstanding boyfriends who enjoy texting until their thumbs ache. They just have a lot to get off their chests, and they dump it all on you—out of pure selfless love. Guys like that must be out there. I just don't happen to know any, or have heard of any.

lisa

A rant via text is just like a rant in spoken language. About two minutes into it, you realized that the person might as well be talking to a mirror, or to a cardboard cutout of Ronald McDonald. He's not really trying to converse with you, or understand you, or find out your feelings for him. He's just pouring out his thoughts and feelings to someone he thinks will listen to them or read them.

Think about the last time you were cornered at a bar by a man who loved the sound of his own voice. He went on and on about whatever was on his mind. The latest *Fast and Furious* movie. Libertarian politics. His bittersweet childhood. His past heartbreaks. Get him going, and he literally will not shut his mouth all night long. He's looking right at you, right into your eyes, as if you are the only person who really understands him. That focus and attention can draw you in. A lot of eye contact seems like intimacy and connection. But chances are, if you went to the bathroom and came back, he would have found another person to lavish his seductive attentions on.

When someone seems to open their heart to you with such a volcanic flow of words and emotion, it creates a false sense of intimacy. I've been there. I've been drawn in by a man who seemed open about his feelings. After the frustration of being with emotionally buttoned-up guys, I was relieved how well, and how much, he expressed himself. Then one day, while listening to him go on for ten minutes on the subject of vegetarian-ism, I realized, *He's not confiding in me.* He was just an open fire hydrant. He wasn't into me per se. He was into talking.

I do believe it's a similar phenomenon when a man is a long-worded texter. The beauty of texting is in the back-and-forth, and in its brevity. You can be witty in few words by text. When someone sends a long text that's not specific and informative, but just a rambling drone about nothing, you have to see it for what it is. You're a captive audience. A forced reader. The text might be to you, but it's not really your concern. It's all about him.

so he's into me . . .
if he sends long-winded multiple texts?

Bro consensus: Here's the thing. When a man pours his heart out by text, he's got a lot of feeling, a lot of emotion. So many things and thoughts and opinions just flow out of him, and he just can't stop the love from coming out. It's a tidal wave of words, and aren't you the luckiest girl in the world to be standing on unprotected ground when it hits? The torrent will sweep you up and carry you away, transport you to . . . Okay, that's enough.

If it looks like bullshit, smells like bullshit, sounds like bullshit, guess what it is?

(133)

kenny

It's bullshit. Nine times out of ten, a guy who waxes poetic to a woman by text is a Player, especially if he does it early on, say, in the first month.

HE TEXTED ME THIS...

.ıll AT&T 🛜   11:12 PM   ▶ ✳ 33% 🔋

[Messages]   [Edit]

Hope you feel better in the morning...I really cannot wait to see you—im anxious I wont lie. You have made my heart race all day and you made my day today. I'm looking forward to us...goodnight and sweet dreams....

Ps. I have a really warm and comfortable chest that is not being occupied by your head right now...hopefully maybe one day i can be your pillow :)

📷 (Text Message)   [Send]

...SO NOW I'M WONDERING?

His friends say he's a bullshitter...my friends say he's a player. But he seems so genuine and sweet to me. Do guys say this stuff to people they're playing? We've never hooked up.

He should save the pillow talk for later in the relationship, when you're actually in bed together.

Players don't necessarily mean to play. They just fall in love hard and fast. (They also fall out just as quickly.) Their texts reflect emotional intensity. He might not even be aware that he's full of it. He believes his own fantasy. When the guy doesn't even realize he's full of it, it's a lot to ask that a girl know it, too.

A non-Player wouldn't dare go overboard with the romantic text language unless he and the girl have been dating for a whi . . . actually, not even then. Using texts to ramble about your feelings is a huge cop-out. If he can't say it in person, he's using the phone as protection. He's afraid to deal with expressing his emotions face-to-face.

The angry text rant—that I understand. Everyone gets pissed off, and ranting takes the edge off it. It can mean he's comfortable sharing it with you. Not that you want to hear it! A furious text about getting cut off in traffic or losing a parking space is not sexy. A polemic about politics? Is there a less sexy subject?

Text ranting at a girl because she pissed you off is another matter. Ironically, this means he does care about you. If he weren't serious about you after you rattled his cage, he wouldn't waste his time typing out a long complaint about it. He'd only spell out his problem if he really needed the woman to understand where he was coming from. But again, it's unlikely he'd text. That'd be passive-aggressive. "

jared

A long text is the conversation equivalent of a long soliloquy, when you have something really important to get off your chest, and you just have to get it all out in one gust or you'll explode. The problem with receiving a long text rant isn't so much that you have to read the whole thing. That would be a pain the ass, because when people are being passionate and expressing strong emotion, they don't bother with autocorrect or use punctuation at all. As rough as it is to comprehend what the person is trying to say, you also have to respond. That puts the receiver in an awkward situation. Your thumbs will be crippled before you finish replying. That simple fact alone, to me, proves that sending a text rant is an inherently selfish act. It's not about sharing. It's not about opening up. It's about one person flinging his or her emotions in the other's face, regardless of how it'll make him or her feel. I can't say if the Ranter is into a girl or not into her. But he is WAY into hearing himself text. If you get off on dating guys who spout endlessly about their hot-button subject of the day, then the Ranter is perfect for you.

As someone who's received text rants, I cringe when I see that it's longer than my phone screen. I just know it'll be painful to read and think, *Oh, shit. She's pissed. Look at this monster.* Even worse? A really short text that reads, "Call me. Now." Then I know I'm in for a voice rant.

brian

I'll agree with what Kenny and Jared said. And I just want to add that content counts, too. Some subjects are too intense for texting (a major fight between couples, politics, religion, football, and in-laws, to mention a few). If a long text about an important subject comes in, the medium makes it seem impersonal. It just creates awkwardness, and makes you wonder why he sent it to you at all. If he wanted to seduce you, he wouldn't go off on her about politics or parking or anything that you might find offensive. Therefore, you have to wonder if he doesn't think of you in that way.

want

A guy who . . .

❋ Understands the basic principles of texting. It's a conversation. A dialogue.

❋ Is a rational person who saves his emotional outbursts for face-to-face encounters when they might actually do him some good. We all love our phones, but there's no substitute for a supportive hug and a trusted friend's sympathetic face when you tell your story.

❋ Appreciates the power of clarity and brevity. You're a busy woman, after all. You can't read long texts all day.

do not want

A bore who . . .

❋ Fails to get the rhythm of texting. He's a soliloquizer, a monologist. The textiverse is his stage, and he's at the center. He expects his audience to read raptly as the verbiage slips from his fingers. And then, he expects a text ovation when he's done.

❋ Is an irrational bloviator who doesn't care about productive discussion or cooling off. He just wants to splatter his opinions and thoughts on his Wall, no matter who gets hit.

❋ Is muddled in confusing verbosity. He'd rather dance around the point than make it.

autocorrect

If you are the long-winded texter, you must have realized by now that men don't often reply to a really long message. Jared confessed that he doesn't even read half of them. He gets tired or bored and his eyes cross midway through and he just stops. The only message a guy will receive about you is that you make his head hurt. Men's eyes glaze over when you rant in person. He's nodding every few minutes, but he's secretly watching the bar TV over your head. Via text, he has the luxury of ignoring your words willfully. He doesn't have to pretend to pay attention.

If you're going to be ignored, wouldn't you rather be ignored in person? Text as few words as possible to arrange a date. Then, spend twenty minutes describing your boss's disgusting eating habits over drinks.

If you're the lucky recipient of a long-winded text, first groan. Then scan. If it makes any sense at all, you can reply to the main point of the message with a short "I hear you" or "Much to say about that F2F tonight." But if the ramble goes nowhere and you simply have no idea how to respond, then don't. You aren't obliged to reply to every text you receive. In fact, a reply text might only prolong his rant. If you ignore it, he'll stew for a bit about what he wrote. Hopefully, he'll feel overcome with embarrassment, shame, and/or regret. After a few hours, he might try to reel it back in by texting, "Never mind." The soul of brevity, you can reply, "K."

the memo

* Some people think texts are the new love letters. Maybe. Mash texts are sugary bonbons, for sure. Just take them with a dash of salt. Cyber sweet talk is one thing. Looking in your eyes and saying the words is another level of intimate.

* When someone sends you an essay, you feel obliged to make the reply that long. But you can always send a one-line response. No matter what he wrote, reply, "So much to say. I'll call you later."

* **Rule of Thumb:** Assume half the Ranter's words are exaggerations, rationalizations, and excuses. How do we know this? Because at least half of what he *says* are exaggerations, rationalizations, and excuses.

blocking etiquette

When to cut someone out of your digital world entirely?

As far as how to do it with proper manners and grace, there are not steps or rules. You just do it. Don't announce it, as in, "One more message, and you're blocked, mister!" Block like a Ninja. Block like a ghost. Do it invisibly, swiftly, and with precision.

On Facebook, you only need to block someone if they're really creepy. A friend of ours told us she had to block a guy once who posted on his Wall a Google map showing every place she'd checked in (tagged photos saying "at this bar," "at this park"). He was stalking her Wall and then making sure she knew it. She got that queasy, scared feeling in her gut, the same one that we all learned to listen to in junior high health class. If you get that evil fluttering (dragonflies?) in the belly when his name comes up on your notifications, then you should block him. If it's just a matter of dislike, you can always Unfriend or put him on Restricted access.

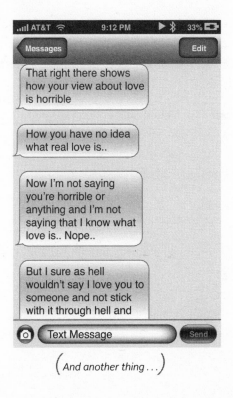

(And another thing . . .)

If he's got your number, then you can program your phone to screen and block his calls and texts. Google "how to block calls" plus the name of your device and the name of your service provider (AT&T, Verizon, T-Mobile) for instructions.

It's usually free for a limited number of incoming phone numbers. If you really feel freaked out, you can change your number, too, usually for a minimal charge. It sucks that some creep would force you into that. It's a pain in the ass. But if you're really and truly disturbed by a guy's texts, changing numbers is worth the inconvenience.

(9)

he sexted

The slippery ins and outs of
naughty texting, and sending and
receiving nekkid pics

the context

He wants to FaceTime with your boobs. (BoobTime: an
app whose time has come?) He might've started out with an
innocent-seeming text like, "What are you wearing?" and
then moved right along to the old favorite, "Send me a photo
of your boobs. PLEEZZZE?" Men are full of "please" and
"thank you" when they want to see your body parts, aren't
they? So polite.

Is there a three-date rule for sexting? Is there any safe way
to send a nude picture without worrying about your boss/
grandmother/priest finding it online?

the subtext

carrie

Seriously? How many celebs have been (or in fairness to those who deny it's them appear to have been) caught with their pants off? Scarlett Johansson, Blake Lively, Kim Kardashian, Miley Cyrus . . . The list seems to go on indefinitely. You are not Jenna Jameson and honestly, do you want to get caught for something like that? It's not like any of the women listed above hahaha'ed when their naked photos were leaked. You do not want to be the girl who makes the classroom or office go silent when she walks through the door. Silence is judgment. FYI: The judgment isn't about how you look. It's about the fact that many thousands of trolls find these sites . . . and you're on one.

The danger of exposure and humiliation is real, and the playing field is far from even. A guy could send a hundred shots of his stuff to his girlfriend. If they had a bitter breakup or he started dating someone else, she might be angry enough to post his pics online. The Internet? Would yawn. The guy would feel nothing but pride about his meat on display like in a butcher shop window. He'd forward the link to all his friends. Men don't get bullied and harassed if their bodies are revealed. It's a total double standard.

Why do women do it at all? We all know the stories. We've seen the *Law & Order* episodes. Some girls think the guy won't like them if they don't send photos. Some do it to lure a man in. Some are exhibitionists. Some do it as a randy bit of foreplay. Most do it, though, because a guy asked them to. He might've had to wear down her reluctance with constant pestering, telling her how sexy it would be, etc. For whatever reason, in the end, she did it to please him.

Women do so much to please men as it is. We try to look good, learn to cook a decent paella, plan vacations, the list goes on. It's completely fair to say, "I do a lot to make you happy. But I'm not doing *that*." If you are leaning toward "Oh, what the hell?" resist. And if you buckle under pressure, for God's sake, don't include your head in the photo.

lisa

A few new apps have come out—and I'm sure a dozen more will, too—that facilitate straight hookups in real time. They're the hetero versions of Grindr. You go to an area of the city and can see all the singles on the service within range. Then you can rate them, essentially hot or not. If a girl you liked also thinks you're hot, you can message each other to hook up. I'm sure there's a lot of rejection for users. Guys don't care. If they approve of a thousand women, and 999 turn them down, there's still one who's willing. I've been told guys *love* those odds. If it's only about sex, any one in a thousand girls will do. A friend said to me, "I'm not going to meet the mother of my children this way."

Most women are not looking for "anyone." We're hoping to find "the One." And when they're in love, he's the only guy in the world. Losing him would be like losing a limb. I remember a friend of mine thought her romantic life was over after a three-month relationship ended. She wailed on the subway over him and truly believed she'd never meet another guy. She told me, "I'll never love anyone as much as I love him!"

That turned out to be the God's honest truth . . . for three weeks. Then she met the man she later married. This is why women wind up texting pictures or Snapchatting in the nude. The fear of losing the only man she'll ever love can lead a woman to do all kinds of insane things. And, if you put it in perspective, sending a photo of your boobs is light work compared to, say, being talked into prostitution or murder. I exaggerate, but not really.

I remember when texting first got big and people went nuts over sexting, the disturbing teen trend. Boys were forwarding girls' sexts to the entire school. Kids can be cruel bullies. And teenage boys are not exactly known for being responsible, sensitive, or thoughtful. For adults, though, most of whom have put in at least one explicit phone conversation in their lives, a few randy sexts are fun, sexy, and no big deal.

God knows what's coming next.

What I'm getting at here: Sexting, sexy photos, random hookup apps, one-night stands, sex clubs, mommy porn, are all available to anyone at the touch of a button. The universe of sexual expression and opportunity is only going to get bigger and weirder as technology advances. You can and should do whatever feels exciting, safe, and fun to you. If what he wants doesn't match up with what you feel comfortable with? It's a sign he's not the right person for you, regardless of how into him you might be. Don't cry on the subway about losing him. Before you know it, another train and another guy will come along.

so he's into me . . .
if he wants to sext and/or get photos?

Bro consensus: He's into your boobs, for sure. Whether he's into your heart and mind is still a giant question mark.

brian

Why do guys ask for photos? I couldn't really tell you specifically. It's just one of those things guys do, and have always done.

Some guys will respect a girl and not save the pictures. But I would say 99 percent save every boob photo they've taken or received on their phone or computer for their own personal record keeping. It's also fairly safe to say that even if the relationship went south, the guy would hold on to that picture.

Personally, I've never asked for photos. It's usually not worth it in the end. If a guy were going to ask for a photo in a non-creepy way, he'd have to wait until after a couple of hookups when everyone is comfortable being naked with each other. Attention, guys: Don't ask for a photo of the boobs until you have seen them already in real life.

HE TEXTED ME THIS...

Send me a picture of u

:)

Oct 29, 2013, 6:15 PM

Hahah no wayyy

Delivered

Please ;)

At least one!

Perhaps of ur pretty little feet :)

Pwease :)

Alright :) I can't wait

I like feet sorry :(sort of

...SO NOW I'M WONDERING?

Do you think he's into me? I'm just not sure cause the last winky face is frowning. Is it weird he would want to see my feet?

Okay, ladies, feel free to send a picture of your foot, your ankle, and your shin. We officially approve of all below-the-knee requests.

If a girl sexted me or sent a picture without being asked for it? I'd react negatively. I'd assume she's done this before, maybe a lot. I know the words *slut* and *slutty* have become politicized. A woman who enjoys sex is not a slut. But someone who doles out naked pictures is probably looser than a girl who wouldn't send them. Having some degree of modesty really matters. Some guys don't care. Players won't get in a serious relationship anyway. They'd get the photo, show all their friends, say, "Yup, that's what a boob looks like," and not give a crap about the girl.

Twenty years ago, a picture of a girl or a sext might have had a bigger impact on a guy. But it's just not going to cause major excitement these days. Frankly, any guy can see a thousand boobs in the click of a mouse. He can have explicit conversations just as easily.

In fact, the biggest danger, from a guy's perspective, is suggesting some kinky scene and getting zero response, like the foot fetishist on the previous page. Feet aren't my thing, but to each their own. A guy likes big bunions. More power to him. If he's got the courage to ask for sexy pinkie-toe photos, he must like and trust you. So you know his heart (at least) is in the right place. He made a pretty intimate admission. Getting zero positive recognition about it would be awkward as hell.

jared

Even if he's totally not into you, he still wants to see your boobs. Every guy wants to see the boobs of every girl on the planet. This can't possibly be surprising. If you live in the world, you know this. Girls walk by guys in the street every day. Those guys don't want to see any of them naked— they want to see *every single one* naked. It's just a fact.

So be aware of that the next time you feel flattered a guy asked to see your boobs. Maybe he's attracted to you. Maybe he just wants to see your boobs because he wants to see every boob in the entire world.

A guy will assume that if you send him sexts and pics, you will move just as fast in person. You can't be one type of girl over text and another in person. If you're a slow boiler sexually, then don't get overheated sextually. Women complain that men send mixed signals. Well, women do, too.

I met this girl and she texted some filthy stuff to me. I went over to her place and we hooked up. When I was going to leave, she said, "You're not sleeping over?"

"Uh, no," I said. To me, it was obviously something fun and spur-of-the-moment. Why would I think different considering what she texted?

Honestly, I haven't done much sexting or photo sharing. Swear to God. Before that one girl I mentioned, I hadn't been involved in that type of relationship. It started when she asked me to download Snapchat. I got the app and she sent a picture. I wasn't quite sure what it was. Let's just say it was an extreme close-up. I knew it'd disappear after four seconds, so I took a quick screenshot of it for more careful study. The next thing I knew, she texted, "You took a screenshot?? You asshole!"

I didn't know Snapchat notified the sender when the receiver took a screenshot. It was embarrassing to get caught. I honestly had no idea. I deleted the screenshot immediately. A dick, though, would keep it and forward it to his friends. From a girl's perspective, in that case, she made the mistake of trusting a dick. It's like being lured into a game of three-card monte. You have to know you're going to lose your money. If you don't, you're naïve or not too bright. When it comes to nudity, you have to be on your guard.

The woman sets the precedent. If you send me a photo of your boobs, it's like a promise that you'll pull up your shirt in real life. I'm not saying the guy has a right to take advantage. Not at all. But I am saying that if the conversation turns sexual in person, you wouldn't be surprised if he made a lunge for you. If the texts turn sexual, when he next sees you, he'll try the same thing. That's why guys love to get naked pictures. They believe it's a green light, that when they see you, it'll get sexual fast, that you've giving them the keys to the kingdom.

Ego alert! Does he think saying "doctor" makes a woman's clothes fly off?

HE TEXTED ME THIS...

U can run my office... If u send a picture haha

Aug 30, 2012, 6:34 PM

Ohhh so mr. big shot over here thinks he'll have his own office one day?

Every doc has an office. That's how this works.

Aug 30, 2012, 6:45 PM

Not if you fail out of school bc your were too busy asking girls to send you nude pics.

Ha. Well played

Text Message

...SO NOW I'M WONDERING?

I like to think I held my ground...but what exactly is he getting at?

People talk about the pitfalls of having sex too soon. What about sexting too soon? It's all too common, or so my friends tell me. You can go from zero to horny too quickly. Let's say it's 1994. You meet someone and it takes a week or more to set up and go on a date.

You have a phone conversation, play voice-mail phone tag (remember phone tag?). Two weeks later, you go on a second date. You know virtually nothing about each other. And you've only really talked in person.

Flash forward to 2014. You meet someone. That night, you both Google each other and check out your respective Facebook Walls. You already know more about each other in a day than you would have over months of dating back in 1994. You start texting immediately, swapping photos and flirting, maybe even borderline sext before your first official date.

What's missing is all the in-between stuff. The waiting for a call and anticipating the date. Wondering if you'll even recognize her, since it's been a week since you saw her last. Anticipation, buildup—the slow parts are gone. Everything moves faster now—and ends a lot faster, too. When in doubt, slow down. Test your feelings. After a few days off from texting with him, do you still feel the same urgency?

kenny

Before you hit Send, be warned: A guy will save every topless shot he gets, and he will show his friends, even if he likes you. He won't think of it as wrong. Due to the accessibility of porn, nude pics are the norm for a certain age group of men. Would you really sext a guy to keep him from dumping you? Have you ever seen an after-school special? Doing something that makes you vulnerable for another person's pleasure is subjecting yourself to the worst kind of exploitation. He'll be glad you sent the picture for him to show all his friends, but he won't like you for it. If you get aggressive and send a photo or sext to seduce him, it might work. You'll get sex. But, again, that's got nothing to do with his liking you, or, frankly, respecting you.

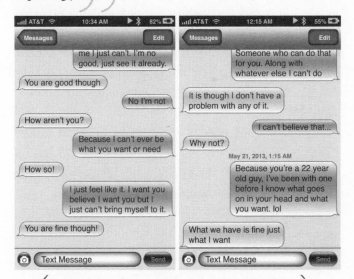

Backstory: He asked her for a threesome. She held her ground, and he seems to be contrite. But can she ever trust him again? Doubtful.

want

Listen, we understand how fun it can be to play lingerie model and Swedish airplane pilot on layover. When you're in the moment, taking revealing photos of each other or sexy selfies is exciting. But it's only fun while it's happening. Like eating a platter of nachos grandes with sour cream, chili, and guac. Once you polish it off or hit Send, there will be consequences. The consequences of those photos might not hit you right away, but they will, and maybe for the rest of your life. (Expect the consequences of the nachos to hit within the hour.)

A lot of women find sexting fun. No question, a man who can be charming and funny while also being seductive and sexy is a catch. Good sext is slightly ironic with the awareness that using phones to excite each other is kind of ridiculous. What's sexy about sexting: It's not the descriptions of body parts and typing what we'd like to do to each other. It's the wit. The humor. The playfulness and emotionally intimate rapport.

We have heard tales of couples with awesome sextual chemistry, but no sexual chemistry. A woman can live on sexual chemistry alone. Red-hot sextual chemistry is just not enough. You're a wise, wonderful woman. Someday, you'll find a man who is as sexy online as he is in person. And then, marry his ass!

She shut him down, but we would have taken it farther than TTYL. We'd have said, "Talk to you never, dipshit," or TTYND.

do not want

＊ A guy who says, "If you don't send me pictures, we're done." Fine. Done. He's blocked, Unfriended, erased from your contacts forever.

＊ A Player who says, "If you loved me, you'd do it." To which you can only reply, "I don't love you, because you're a douchebag."

autocorrect

When push comes to shove, you could promise him the keys to the kingdom a million times over by text. But a text is not a binding sexual contract. You can always say, "Actually, no." It's a woman's prerogative to change her mind, especially about sex or sext. You do not have to go through with anything. If you are already in a situation where things moved too quickly, what started as playful flirting turned into full-blown sexting, and he's heading over right now, cut it off before he rings the buzzer. Go ahead and text, "Things moved too fast. I got carried away. Let's put this off tonight. Sorry." He might be pissed off. But a gentleman will understand, and might even be a little relieved.

the memo

✳ Ever heard of revenge porn? It's the disturbing practice of men posting naked pictures of their ex-girlfriends on websites. Some truly evil pigs include names, e-mail addresses, and phone numbers along with the pictures. Women have been harassed and humiliated, and had their privacy violated by the men they once adored. Yeah. Doesn't get worse on the Internet than this stuff. It should be illegal. It should be a crime. A fitting punishment: boiling in a stew of his own fluids. Some victims are fighting for their rights, and for justice. The legal system hasn't yet caught up with certain vile aspects of life online, though. The ONLY WAY to make sure revenge porn never ever, ever happens to you? Don't take naked pictures.

✳ **Rule of Thumb:** If you wouldn't put the picture in a frame for your mother, DON'T SEND IT.

✳ Your 2,729 Facebook Friends prove the point: This guy is not the only man in your social network. His request for wallpaper boobs is not the last text you will ever receive from a guy. There will be other, more worthy men who don't push you to do anything you're not comfortable with.

✳ When sexting, remember, it's the playfulness that's really a turn-on. The body parts, insert tab A into slot B, etc., aren't as sexy as humor and wit. Even when sexting, keep it fun and light.

✳ If it should come to pass that a sext of a photo with your name on it is forwarded around or put up on a website, the best defense is a strong offense. Saying, "Damn, I look good," will be psychologically healthier for you than feeling shame. The shame isn't yours. It's his, for posting it.

(10)

he linked

If his Facebook Wall is a glimpse inside
his virtual home, his links are a much
closer look at his bookshelf, music
collection, and closet. It's the next layer
of disclosure in the benign stalking
universe that is the Internet. So do you
two link up, or is he coming off like the
missing link?

the context

Guys love to send links to their favorite websites, articles, videos, Flickr account, Tumblr blogs. You should pay attention to his links. It's the modern equivalent of perusing a guy's CD collection or his bookshelf for clues about his personality. You can use his URLs to assess his taste, affiliations, interests, and general life philosophy. Each one tells you a little about him—and about how he feels about you.

Believe us, you want to know what he's into, besides you. Despite the old saying that opposites attract, couples should have a few things in common. A band. A favorite author. A pet cause. For that matter, a pet! If you can't stand each other's music or shows, then you're going to fight about what to stream on Netflix or for control of the friggin' remote. Agree to disagree? Not as elegant a solution as you might think. You'll spend nights in staring at screens in separate rooms. If for nothing else, shared interests and passions give you stuff to talk about a few years down the road, when you've heard all of each other's stories and have logged a thousand dinners across the table from each other. The chatter doesn't stay fresh and bouncy forever, you know.

The upshot is that, on entering a relationship, a wise woman checks to see if her links are in sync with those of her man. If he sends you the URL of a vintage Motörhead vid, and you love Selena Gomez? That might be a problem. Just saying.

the subtext

lisa
The other extreme is a guy who sends lots of photos of kittens in baskets, or a link to a streaming video feed of cavorting baby foxes or a live panda birth at the Beijing Zoo. Super-adorable links from a guy might be

more questionable than the gross-out videos and articles about obscure horror film directors from the 1970s. Call me old-fashioned, but cutesy from a guy is a turnoff. One text that came into HeTexted was a guy sending his new girlfriend a photo of polar bears. Was he an environmentalist? Did he think she'd be in "awwww" of it—and him? Or is he just really into polar bears? The white fur, black noses, and such? She had no idea what to make of the photo.

A link can seem like the digital equivalent of avant-garde art. You don't know what it means, but you can't stop thinking about it. A guy once sent me a link to fifteen photos of cats and dogs licking themselves. What to make of *that*? Was it supposed to be humor, or a hint? And a hint regarding *what*, exactly? A few rules of thumb: Him sending you a link about something he knows you're into, as if he were doing some clicking on your behalf, is a good sign. A link to another girl's Tumblr blog, with the message "Whaddaya-think about her? She's so hot!" isn't a good sign. Don't fall into the "He's making me jealous" trap. That's what women do to keep hope alive.

so he's into me . . .
if he sends me a lot of links?

Bro consensus: http://hetexted.com/bros

brian

Any article exchanged between the two of you should refer back to a previous conversation, like an inside joke. If a guy sends you a link to something you've talked about before, that's usually flirting. I highly recommend sending relevant links to a guy you like. The best way for you to flirt and make him realize that you're interested—and interesting in general—is to pay attention to your conversations and conveniently come across a pertinent article. Guys like that. They like that you were actually listening, and that you might like the same things. Guys feel a lot of pressure about talking to girls. If he had a reliable subject to bring up that didn't bore you to tears, he'd be so grateful to know it. So keep links relevant. Share common areas of interest. But not too many! More than two links a week is embarrassing, in either direction.

I know that it used to be a declaration of love for a guy to make a mix CD of his favorite songs for a woman. Nowadays, it's kind of awkward to share a Vimeo, as in, "Hey. I love this band and hope you will, too. Check it out!" It sounds like computer-generated spam, the opposite of personal and relevant. Better to send an article about a band you talked about, or rare concert footage of the singer dropping his pants onstage. Something funny or obscure. If he does this, he is *definitely* into you. He listened to you, took time to unearth the video, and wants to keep the conversation going.

Guys also use links to try to get a direct response. If you want to go to a restaurant with him, send a Yelp review. Interested in a movie date? Send a Rotten Tomatoes page and hope he can take a not-at-all-subtle hint. It's making a direct point without having to say it directly. Guys will identify and appreciate the effort. A good guy will reply, "Wanna go?" A jerk will just send the note, "Sounds cool," and leave it up to her to do the official asking.

jared

As a comedian (have I mentioned that I'm a comedian?), I see the humor in sending a random photo or weird link. The more obscure and mysterious the better. If she is totally baffled by it, good. She'll have to get in touch with me for an explanation.

I agree with Brian: The keyword about links is *relevant*. On a recent date, the girl talked about a writer she liked. Then she sent me the author's Amazon link, with the note, "She's so funny." I might never click the link or read the writer's third-wave feminist humor essay collection, but I appreciate the girl's effort. Her link had a purpose, was relevant to our conversation, and was revealing about her. If she just randomly shared or forwarded an article someone sent to her that didn't touch on something we'd discussed or something she knew I was into, it would be just some BS excuse to make contact. That feels stalkerish.

Links serve a purpose, which is to further a conversation, share something about yourself, and find common interests. You don't have to click through. How many times have you received a link, read the first and last sentences, and sent a vague reply about the last sentence? Many times. I don't have time to read every article! But if I do make a comment, I want to give the appearance that I have. This cheat hasn't backfired yet. It could at any time, and I won't be prepared in the least. I'm not planning that far ahead. But, generally speaking, I wouldn't read too much into a guy commenting on a link you sent. He probably hasn't read it. He's just being polite.

The avant-garde text: You have no idea what it's supposed to mean, but you can't stop thinking about it.

> But, I still prefer soft tacos to hard tacos.

> U discust me

> D

> IM SORRY

> Its good lol k talk to u later going to bed ill leave u with a picture of a finger

> night 😔

kenny

I have to weigh in here: If a guy sends you that video of *Big Booty Bitches* with the note, "This made me think of you," that would be extremely weird. But if he sent it to fifty people, with the note "OMFG," it'd be kind of funny.

(167)

want

A link that . . .

＊ Is relevant to conversations you're had with him.

＊ Indicates you share common tastes and interests.

＊ Makes you smile, laugh, or cry in a good way.

do not want

A link that . . .

＊ Is bafflingly irrelevant to your conversations and has nothing to do with you. He could have sent the same link to a thousand other people, and maybe did.

＊ Proves that you have nothing in common, be it interests, taste, sense of humor, or basic human decency.

＊ Makes you want to call the cops, run for the bathroom to puke, or scars you for life.

autocorrect

Your potential as his girlfriend is only as strong as your weakest link. If you send random stuff to clog his in-box, he won't think, *This is the girl for me.* He'll think, *What the hell is this now?* If at all in doubt of a link's worthiness, don't send.

the memo

❋ Don't assume he actually reads/views your links. Dude has hours and hours of YouTube videos about skateboard accidents to screen and can't read every article about Alanis Morrissette and the twenty-year anniversary of *Jagged Little Pill*. If he sends back a comment, "Great article!" don't quiz him on it. It'll get awkward.

❋ The clicking life of men takes them to some strange and dark corners of the Internet. His tolerance for gross-out and bizarre information might be a lot higher than yours. Don't judge. Just shield your eyes.

❋ Incidentally, make sure you clear your browser history every day. Just because.

(11)

we dated

You use the phone to meet, flirt, get to know each other, and arrange the date. But what about while you're on the date itself? If you leave your phones on the table, the entire textiverse might as well be crowded around it, too.

the context

So you're finally on a date! Mazel tov! L'chaim! All the flirty texting, "liking," and linking has culminated in a face-to-face meeting. You relied on devices to get to this place (maybe literally with Google maps). But you're here now. Devices are no longer needed. So why can't we seem to let them go, or put them away?

We're all guilty of infractions: Updating your status while he's in the bathroom. Tweeting a picture of the two of you taken dutifully by the solicitous waiter. Tweeting a photo of your meal. Rehashing the date later that night on Facebook. In-real-life dates still manage to find their way online, even while the date is actually happening. Not cool, or sexy. Sorry.

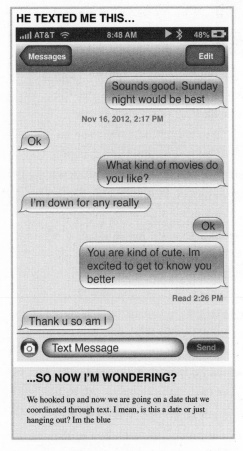

HE TEXTED ME THIS...

.ull AT&T 📶   8:48 AM   ▶ ✳ 48% 🔋

< Messages   Edit

> Sounds good. Sunday night would be best

Nov 16, 2012, 2:17 PM

Ok

> What kind of movies do you like?

I'm down for any really

> Ok

> You are kind of cute. Im excited to get to know you better

Read 2:26 PM

Thank u so am I

📷 Text Message   Send

...SO NOW I'M WONDERING?

We hooked up and now we are going on a date that we coordinated through text. I mean, is this a date or just hanging out? Im the blue

Pre-date texting don't: Playing your cards before the game has started. You can tell him he's cute after the movie when he kisses you good night.

the subtext

carrie

Why do we feel compelled to post how great the salmon is, or take a selfie while he's in the bathroom with the comment, "Two drinks deep!"? Do our 843 friends need to know that he likes his steak medium rare?

Phones help us kill time when we're bored, stay in touch, get information, etc. But in a tense situation—we can agree that all dates are a bit tense, at least at first—we use them as security blankets. Our phones will protect us and keep us safe. Our friends are only a click away. We're not vulnerable and anxious as long as we have our phones.

Baby steps. First, silence the phone. Then, gently put it down. After you catch your breath, slowly put the phone *away*. Now direct your attention to the man you've been so excited and nervous to meet. It's called *being* in the moment, in the present time. Easier said than done. Our minds race ahead to the future or fall back to the past. It could be due to the wide corpus callosum, the fibrous band that connects the two hemispheres of our brain. On women, it's wider than on dudes, which is why we can multitask (seriously; look it up) and time-travel in our heads while holding down a conversation.

In the digital era, it's also hard to *stay* in the moment, in the present place, metaphorically. Facebook isn't a real place. But if you're on Facebook, you're not in the restaurant, even if you're checking in on Facebook, saying that you're currently at the restaurant. Even when we're having a good time on a date, we feel pulled to that other place, thinking, *I need to tell my friends what a good time I'm having.* We can barely wait until the bread basket arrives to refresh our News Feed and sneak a peek at it while he butters up. That, ladies, is a major turnoff. If a guy did it, you'd probably reach for your phone to post an update about your outrage.

I cringe when the girl who sat behind me in European history posts, "Just had the best. Dinner. Ever. #mesagrill with @bigjay Thank you, babe!" Babe? She barely knows Big Jay. They were on a blind first date! She'd been updating every ten minutes all day long about her choice of outfit ("Sexy mini or keyhole maxi? I look hot in both!"), the traffic ("Cab to Mesa Grill LOL #spoiled"), and an under-the-table update when he ordered wine ("$100 bottle of Merlot. #slurp").

My policy for this: zero tolerance. I might have to Unfriend this girl . . . if I didn't enjoy mocking her so much. Relentless upbeat updates, to me, sound fake and insecure. She seems to be seeking approval from her friends, rather than focusing on the only person whose opinion matters in the moment: her date. Updating or texting her friends might make her feel better. She's getting the feedback she needs so badly. And the guy? His date is blown. (And he dropped a bundle at Mesa Grill #nexttimejustdrinks.) An itchy Facebook finger is an "insecurity tell." Even a minidress can't make desperation look sexy. If Big Jay saw those posts about him and their date, he'd never text her again.

I do empathize with European-history girl. She's just a woman of her time. Circa 2002, when you had to dial into AOL Instant Messenger via modem, things were more straightforward. Snail's-pace slow, but straight. That was a magical era of ;) emoticons and Blink-182-friendly MySpace profiles. When a boy wanted to ask you on a date, he called your landline and used his actual voice to say, "Want to get dinner?" You used your actual voice to say, "Sure!" You might've called a friend for a pre-date pep talk, and then the postmortem. But that was it.

It's no wonder we overthink the heck out of everything, because we can solicit hundreds of opinions on our every move. We're addicted to reassurance and feedback. It's not enough that a guy tells you, "You look nice tonight." You have to tell the world (your world) what he said instantly, or it's like it didn't happen.

I'm sorry to say that this problem is ours. I'm 110 percent guilty of this. God KNOWS I have tweeted the drinks on the bar before. And even used a filter. I'm not saying we shouldn't do this, period; I'm just saying it shouldn't consume the majority of the date. A girl posts about her date because she's excited and wants to share. She might as well be saying to him, "I'm into you," if she weren't furiously typing.

lisa

The levels of disconnect can get pretty deep if you text while on the date. I have a friend who didn't realize how far into cyberspace she'd fallen until she got this text: "Your pasta is getting cold." It was from her date! The waiter brought her dinner, and she hadn't realized. Real-time update: You suck.

I heard another story about a woman who was texting her date while walking across the street to the restaurant where he was waiting for her. Her head down, typing, "Be right th—" She didn't see the taxi.

The date watched the accident from the bar window. He ran outside. She was okay. Just a bruised rib. The cabdriver took them to the hospital. They had their first date in the ER. Meet-cute story? If you think "cute" means "almost getting killed." Keep your eyes on the road, ladies! Don't walk and text! Don't date and text!

Why do women commit this cyber sin of compulsively one-step removing themselves from the date by texting about the date? It's so meta, my head is about to explode. Tough love, ladies: It's a form of narcissism. If others don't know what's happening in your life, is it really happening? Our instant-gratification, feedback-addicted culture reinforces this behavior. I mean, if you can get five "likes" on every post, why not keep updating? (Because the 829 friends who didn't "like" are beyond annoyed with you.) At fifty, will you need friends to validate your outfit choice? Someday—soon—the confidence has to come from within. Break the habit of over-updating, especially on a date. Trust that you are as lovely and charming as your friends say you are.

so he's into me . . .
if he texts while on a date?

Bro consensus: What was the question? Just give me one second. I have to answer this . . . Okay, where did I grow up? Hold that thought, I just got a text . . . two seconds . . . So, you were saying? What? Oh shit, there it goes again . . .

brian

I'm not theoretically opposed to phones on the table. At a business lunch, it's like a scripted ballet. As soon as the credit card is taken away by the waiter, everyone checks his or her phone. The business is concluded, so it's appropriate to take a quick look at what you missed. It would be terrible to check your phone in the middle of a meeting. You might as well text your lunch companion, "I didn't want the stinkin' job anyway."

I think people on a date should show each other the same courtesy and respect. I get all the furious texting and checking your notifications that went into getting you here. But now you're on the date! Time to put your phone away and get on with the F2F you worked so hard to arrange. Don't touch the phone for the length of the date, from the minute you enter the restaurant until you're back home again. If you bring him home with you, don't look at your phone until he's asleep or gone the next day. What is so important that it can't wait? Really. Unless it's a genuine crisis, just put it off and live your real life.

Obviously, this is a rule for early dates, before you know each other well and are an established couple. It's still rude to sit across from your girlfriend and text other people. A text checker is essentially saying the two-sentence message is more important than you.

As much as you are with this person, you are not mentally there. You're thinking about a message you want to come in or send about something else. If you glance at the phone or check it in front of your date, you appear to be interested in the sports score that popped up on your screen. Maybe you are. But it's still rude to act like it.

If one of you takes a bathroom break, I guess it's okay to quickly check your phone. A lot of people will update their status while the other person is in the bathroom. That's not okay. Say he was checking his News Feed in there, and saw that you updated about him? The entire tone of the date will change, and not for the better.

Now, I realize that some younger people

will use their phone to fill a lull in conversation, to take it out to show the other person a video or a photo to build a bridge to a new topic of discussion. That's definitely fair. But you shouldn't have your phone out in the first place. It's one thing to say, "Oh, you have to see these photos," and take it out. But it should be in your pocket, not on the table, before you do. A phone on the table is a distraction. If it vibrates or lights up, you're taken out of the moment. A date just can't get going that way.

kenny

If a guy takes a call on a date, it better be very bad news, like someone died. Or very good news, like he was just elected president. Otherwise, his picking up the phone and saying hello might as well be him saying, "I'm not into you." I'd cut some slack for a guy under twenty. He might not know what he's doing and take a call. It's awkward and stupid, especially if he likes you. He might even think (God help him) it's cool, like he's in demand and you'll notice that about him. Men over twenty have figured out that, on a date, you want the man 100 percent focused on you. You dressed up for it. You listened to his stories. You've got some of your own to tell. The two of you look at each other and pay attention to each other. That's a date.

What's not a date: The guy holding up his finger and saying, "Gotta take this," or thumbing a text quickly while smiling and laughing over something that came in, and will remain a mystery to the tight-lipped grinning lady across the table. "

jared

Yeah, the friggin' Millennials. They don't have a clue. I read recently that Millennials are known for looking at their phones in the middle of a job interview—and that they blame the economy for their high unemployment rate. I hope the boss sent a text that said, "BTW, you're NOT hired."

I agree with Brian on the working/dating comparison. Dating is like a job interview. The job is being each other's boyfriend or girlfriend (it's good work, the best kind). The phone should not be out on the table. If a girl checks her phone when I'm interviewing her for the position, I think, *Unqualified. She's bored by me after one drink.* I need a candidate who finds me interesting enough to talk for the length of an entire meal. So should anyone! It's not too much to ask. Show some restraint. It's offensive to whip out your phone on a date. It shouldn't happen at all if you're having a good time.

At some point, one of you is going to go to the bathroom. Take a look at your alerts if you must, but not until he's out of sight, or you are. Updating from the bathroom? Your friends are dying to know if he chews with his mouth closed? They can't wait another twenty minutes? That's pathetic. It's like when you marry a woman, you marry her family. When you date a woman who texts compulsively, you're taking two hundred of her Friends out to dinner. I can't afford that!

Nine times out of ten, it's not going to work out with the person you're dating—and that's okay. Most relationships fail (unless you've married every guy you went to dinner with). But a woman updating about the date while it's happening *dooms* it to fail. You can't have perspective on a tornado while inside the eye of the storm. You have to wait until you're outside it to see it. Commenting on a date in progress is like writing the story of a relationship that doesn't exist yet. By doing that, you already have your ending. And it isn't happy.

Women do this all the time. They meet

a guy and start constructing the plot. They post, "I met the One." He's the man of their dreams. If they put that status up, and the guy sees it on her Wall, he knows she has no sense of discretion, that her expectations are unrealistic, and that she's turned him into some kind of Prince Charming. He might scroll back over the past six months to see she's posted about quite a few other "the Ones." Men want to be liked for who they are. This woman doesn't even know this guy. She's constructed an idea of him based on a fantasy. This definitely qualifies as "she crazy" behavior. Unless he's a creep who sees her as a sure thing, he might not ask her out again.

want

A date who . . .

* Looks you in the eye.

* Hangs on your stories.

* Asks you questions about yourself.

* Is curious about what you think of him.

* Is flirty yet respectful.

* Is solicitous without being chauvinistic.

(183)

❋ Was once a bad boy and is now a mensch who's learned well from his mistakes.

❋ Has a loving relationship with his mother, not too creepy and close or resentful and distant.

❋ Loves his work, but doesn't live to work.

❋ Ideally, is creative and financially comfortable.

❋ Dresses well without being foppish or precious.

❋ Er, we could go on for quite a while here . . .

do not want

A dud who . . .

❋ Is more interested in his News Feed than in the sexy intelligent woman across the table from him (you).

❋ Says, "I hope you don't mind, I need to check the hockey score." Hockey? It'll probably be the same score in an hour when the date's over. But whatever. You do mind, regardless of the sport.

❋ Doesn't send you a text within forty-eight hours of the date. Even if it doesn't work out in the long run, it's rude to drop off the face of the earth. Just two words mean so much: "Thank you." You could never hear from him again, and you wouldn't hate him.

autocorrect

Are you a charter member of Women Who Update Too Much? Like any bad habit, smoking, nail-biting, saying "like" every other word ("And I'm, like, ewww, you know? Like, gross! It's, like, sickening to, like, listen to . . ."), the habit of compulsive posting must be broken. Count your updates, and reduce your daily total a bit each per day until you get down to three max. One selfie a day is more than enough. Slowly diminish your jones for retweets. And then, on Date Day, you won't have withdrawal spasms about leaving your phone in your purse.

the memo

✳ Think of the phone on a date as a grenade. As soon as you press a button, your potential relationship is blown to bits.

✳ If the conversation stalls and he resorts to showing you a video or a funny photo, it can be a cute way to get things going again. That's not necessarily a black hole. It could be a bridge. But if you spend all night staring at a phone, it's a bridge to nowhere.

✳ The only time it is absolutely encouraged to take out your phone on a date is to take a photo of another couple using their phones on a date. Add the caption Grown-Ass Couple Too Lame to Talk to Each Other on a Date. Post it on Facebook, watch it go viral, bond with the guy over your insta-fame and . . . meme.

the post-date text

The date happened. Now what? Text a thank-you or just wait for him to contact you again?

Our friend Sally jumped the gun on a post-date follow-up. The predate arrangements were made by e-mail, so Sally didn't have his cell number beforehand. As they walked outside the restaurant after a good first date, he gave her his phone number. They kissed good night. He turned to walk toward his car. Sally called his number ON THE SPOT.

He answered, "Sally?"

"Uh, just checking to make sure it's your real number," she said, and hung up.

She could see his frown from across the parking lot.

The next day, he texted, "I don't like being thought of as a liar. It was nice to meet you. Good luck."

A kiss-off. She never heard from him again. A lot of you are probably shaking your head, thinking, *Who DOES that?* You do, Little Miss Perfect! We all do. Post-date paranoia is a bona fide psycho-syndrome (seriously; look it up; actually, don't). The night Carrie met her husband, she asked for his number and then pulled the "Can you spell your full name?" because, well, that's a polite way of saying, "I've already forgotten your last name." So, when he did text the next day (bless his soul), she knew it was for real.

Where this could have gone wrong: if Carrie called the number when he was still standing there, and his phone didn't ring. Now THAT would have felt like crap.

HE TEXTED ME THIS...

> Hey. I take it last week was a little too far? lol

No just been sick still and busy with work though I probably shouldn't be working

Was it too much for you? I'm sorry I didn't intend to push!

> No I just wanted to make sure you didn't get the wrong impression about me...I hope you feel better

...SO NOW I'M WONDERING?

He's been wanting a relationship with me for a while. We live far away but agreed to meet up a month ago. I didn't hear much back. Then he asked if we could have sex. I said no at first. Two weeks ago one thing led to another...and this is the last he's said. It's been 8 days now. Granted he is extremely busy. Should I be concerned or let it slide?

Post-date texting don't: Ask for a rejection. Looks like he got what he wanted, and moved on. She already knew it, but had to text to confirm. If you think he's blowing you off, ladies, he probably is. Good riddance, and NEXT.

brian

After a date, my advice is to not text or update about it at all. There is just no reason to report the news. Send private messages to your friends about it. But if you post, "I had the best date tonight!" and the guy sees it, he won't be happy. Men just don't like their personal lives broadcasted publicly. He might assume the girl is an over-sharer and lives her entire life on the Internet. She lacks wisdom about when to keep important things and intimate relationships private. That's a huge turnoff. It could mean the difference between getting a second date or not.

jared

Total agreement about the post-date update. You put a potential relationship at risk. As for the post-date text, I always send something. It's like writing a thank-you note, even if you hate the gift. It's just what you do. If I want to see her again, I write, "I had a great time last night. We should do it again very soon." If I never want to see her again, I write, "I had a good time last night. Thanks for coming out."

If I hear back from the girl I liked, I'll immediately start asking her questions and continuing the conversation. If I hear back from the girl I didn't like, I phase her out with short replies until I don't reply at all.

Some women have asked me why I send a post-date text to a girl I'm not into. It's a courtesy. If you met someone at a party or work event, you shake hands, say, "It was great to meet you," and both of you understand you'll probably never talk to or see each other again. You say the courteous thing because we abide by the social contract of not being complete assholes to each other. Does a guy have to be a complete asshole to a girl so she gets he's not into her? Sometimes the message doesn't get through otherwise.

Girls read into a guy's words when they should look only at his actions. If he writes, "Talk to you soon," a woman should reasonably expect to hear from him. But if he never calls? She has confirmation the "talk soon" was a gentle blow-off. If he does call, the "talk soon" was the gospel truth. Either way, if you can wait a few days, you'll have a definitive answer.

I'm sure a lot of guys don't bother sending a post-date thank-you to a girl they don't particularly like. But if he does send a note, reply, "I had a nice time, too. It was a lot of fun. Let me know when you are free to do it again." It's not the Dark Ages. You could ask him on the second date yourself. But a guy likes having the ball in his court. If he wants to see you again, he'll ask. If he doesn't, he won't.

It's absolutely fine for a woman to send the first post-date text. "Thanks, I had a great time last night." That's it. Leave it up to him to continue the conversation from there. A second date should be made in the same way as the first date. Look, when you're an established couple, you know you'll make all the plans and be in complete control of your social life. Just let him be in control of the first few dates.

(12)

he ☺

He texted emojis of a car, an ice-cream cone, and a heart. Does that mean he loves Dairy Queen drive-thru, or you?

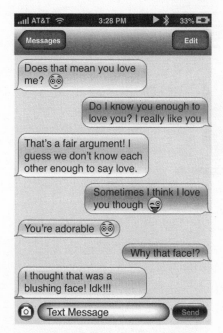

Watch out. Using emojis is like playing with a loaded gun. One slip of the finger, and it's all over.

the context

One of the things you love about him? His smile. He's got so many different variations. Sometimes he smiles and winks, or smiles with his tongue out, or with googly eyes or . . . Hey, wait a tick. It's not his actual face. He just really, really likes emojis. (*Emoji* is the Japanese word for what we, Americans, used to call emoticons, back in the Renaissance of the Internet, aka 2003. Of course, now, emojis are thousands of faces, symbols, and icons that seem to be replacing words and letters.)

the subtext

carrie

Is it ever appropriate to use fifteen smiley faces before and after each line of text? Is it cute or lazy to send an emoji of a slice of pizza to say, "I'm hungry. Let's grab a slice"? Yeah, we get it that some emojis are funny and ironic. But you can irony a thing to death until it's reborn to earnestness. And then he stops being a cool dude and turns into a man-boy who likes smiley faces. How to know if his use of emojis is legit, and whether the symbols he sends have any special meaning for you and only you?

lisa

This might sound unfair, but I think it's abominable when a man uses emoticons or emojis. They come off as super cheesy (especially the pizza slice!). I don't know a politically correct way to say this, but outside, in the larger world (not America or Japan), people hardly use them at all. Sending a thumbs-up symbol seems normal in the United States. Abroad? Thumbs DOWN.

I personally hate them. But then again, I am Australian. I'd rather a guy send, "Beer me," that an emoji of a frosty glass. I can read. I'm not a three-year-old who needs pictures. It's a blackball to me, a blue balls for him. A man once asked me to dinner and included an emoji of a smiley face with hearts for eyes. I replied, "You are a man, right? Not a woman with the name Stanley?" If I wanted a man to be cute and sweet, I'd date my neighbor's shih tzu. (Manly facial hair? Check. Keeps himself clean. Check. Human? Damn! I knew there was something wrong.)

so he's into me . . .
if he emojis a thumbs-up?

Bro consensus: The three of us aren't such big fans of hearts and flowers and winking smiley faces. Some of us do, however, appreciate old-fashioned emoticons for their cleverness.

kenny

I personally don't see how you can use emojis non-ironically. But a lot of guys do it (and overdo it). The idea is to save time and use a symbol to convey an idea succinctly. Funnily enough, I think emojis are even harder to decipher than words. Everyone uses them differently, and there isn't a common meaning or interpretation for what they mean. Fifteen smiley faces in a row? It could mean he's daydreaming about ice cream. It could mean he fell asleep with his thumb on the key. I'd say the guy really likes you but is currently at a first-grade reading level. He might not have anything to say. So in place of words, he decides to embarrass himself with pictures instead. "Girls love this!" he'll think as he hits Send. Sad, misguided bastard.

brian

Symbols can be funny within a certain context. I send them to good friends, but only in a joking, stupid way. If it's just between friends, the goofier the better. For a girl I'm just starting to get to know, I would never send one. It's too early for that level of joking around. She might take a smiley face seriously, or think I do. You have to establish comic rapport first. As you progress as a couple and get to know each other, then the flirtier emojis are the totally crazy ones. A friend of mine asked her husband, "How was your day?" and he sent her back an emoji of a pile of shit with eyes. Now that's a healthy, happy relationship. Even when he was complaining about his day, he elicited a laugh from his wife.

jared

Like most guys, I don't find emojis an important issue. I know some girls love them and do, like, ten hearts in a row, or ten V-finger peace signs. Crap like that. Guys who put up ten hearts in a row are either gay or super-ironic hipsters who are probably gay and don't know it yet. I guess I can see a scenario when a straight guy would send them to his friends to screw with them. But to a girl he's trying to sleep with? Hearts do not say, "I want you." They say, "I love bunnies."

Guys like to keep their cards pretty tight. They're not going to give you any reason to doubt their sexual orientation at all. They also don't want to come off as needy or clingy. I can't say exactly why sending emojis seems needy and clingy. I might be flashing back to a horrible fling that I've forcibly blocked from my consciousness. Using symbols instead of words is gimmicky. When I receive them, it's a turnoff. It seems desperate to be cute. I don't want a girl to think of me that way (not that she would). So I don't take that chance. I do think a wink emoticon sent by a girl is flirtatious. If she sends me a bunch of winks, I'm taking that only one way. I'll wink back, even, right after pigs fly out of my ass.

Effective use of ironic winking: This is totes adorbs. Who knew "I like math" could be flirty, and that "I like lunch" could be charming?

want

An emoji that . . .

* Is used either ironically or affectionately.

* Is gender-neutral or decidedly masculine.

* Makes you laugh or deepens your understanding of his message.

do not want

An emoji that . . .

* Is used with such squeaky-clean earnestness, you feel dirty.

* You wouldn't dare show your friend, because she'd say, "He's gay?"

* Makes you cringe and blush with embarrassment—for him.

autocorrect

Just be warned that overuse of emojis, as if they really are replacing your use of language and the ability to express a thought or emotion that's more complicated than evil eyebrows, makes you seem insubstantial and very young. If you want a man to take you seriously, then at least use something that shows him you're a serious person, like . . .

the memo

❋ Oh, go ahead and have your fun! Emojis are a trend. Like all trends, it'll pass. So enjoy them while you can. Remember, if you put up the symbols of a pair of shoes, a lipstick, and a thumbs-up, you will come across as a bit superficial and maybe a little illiterate.

❋ Next time a guy asks you to send him a photo of your boobs or butt, send this: (.)(.) and (_|_) ☺☺☺☺☺☺☺

emojis we'd like to see

Calling all artists!!! In the spirit of pictures being worth a thousand words, we thought it'd be cool to come up with symbols that are worth five or six words. Sadly, we're not very good at drawing. But you are! We'd like to solicit some new emojis to use on HeTexted. If you have any brilliant ideas to illustrate the following ideas, please send them to us and we'll post them on HeTexted.com.

1. You smell bad.

2. You make my heart melt.

3. I never want to see you again.

4. First-date jitters.

5. Third-date jitters.

6. One-night-stand-worthy.

7. Don't talk about your ex.

8. He wants me to meet his mother.

(13)

he lied

He said he was staying in, but his friend tagged a photo of him at a bar less than a mile *from your apartment*. Does he lie to protect your feelings and/or does he think you're a moron??

the context

Do you cut him slack for cyber fibbing, believing that telling a lie by text isn't the same thing as a guy lying right to your face? We call bullshit on that. A lie is a lie is a lie, no matter how it was delivered. That's our version of Truth. Guys? They believe in the Half-Lie Theory. If it's a text, with abbreves and such, hardly any letters, then it's hardly a lie. Optimistically, their glass is half-full of deceit. If a man lies via text, can you trust him again?

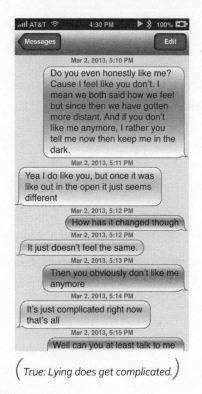

Mar 2, 2013, 5:10 PM

Do you even honestly like me? Cause I feel like you don't. I mean we both said how we feel but since then we have gotten more distant. And if you don't like me anymore, I rather you tell me now then keep me in the dark.

Mar 2, 2013, 5:11 PM

Yea I do like you, but once it was like out in the open it just seems different

Mar 2, 2013, 5:12 PM

How has it changed though

Mar 2, 2013, 5:12 PM

It just doesn't feel the same.

Mar 2, 2013, 5:13 PM

Then you obviously don't like me anymore

Mar 2, 2013, 5:14 PM

It's just complicated right now that's all

Mar 2, 2013, 5:15 PM

Well can you at least talk to me

(*True: Lying does get complicated.*)

the subtext

carrie

The story that springs immediately to mind: My friend Sarah (she'd shave my eyebrows off if I used her real name; not the same friend as Sally, either) was seeing this guy for around three weeks when they hit a road bump. It was a Saturday, and he said he'd text her when he knew what his plan was. Okay, fine. By 11 P.M., she hadn't heard from him. The only logical step was to casually check his Twitter. (No, she didn't follow him on Twitter, and yes, she checked it regularly. Thanks for turning us all into second-degree stalkers, World Wide Web.) Only five minutes before, he'd tweeted "Not even midnight and the Back Room is packed." The Back Room was a popular sports bar in the area. They actually met there.

Sarah decided her best bet was to text him, asking, "You out yet?" She hoped to get the same location he'd just shared with his sixty-four followers on Twitter.

He replied, "Yup, headed to Back Room, stop by if you want."

She replied, "You're an effing liar asshole!" Um, no. She didn't really. But she was thinking it, really hard, while holding her phone. Meanwhile, "if you want," he wrote?!

The story didn't end with her quiet indignation. She was a woman of action. She wanted to go to the Back Room. A group of us went with her for moral support. She wound up going home with him that night. In hindsight, we were the Worst Friends Ever. Friends don't let friends go home with guys who lie by text. Surprise! Sarah and this guy didn't work out. They established a pattern.

He lied, she tracked him down, they met up, and . . . scream.

When a guy likes you, he's going to text you at 9 P.M. and say, "I'm at the Back Room." You will not have to Nancy Drew that shit. But more importantly, he won't play you for a fool by lying so obviously.

Another friend, named Stacy (we like the letter *S* for Suedonyms), got a long love-letter text from a guy. She was kind of swept off her feet by it. A mutual friend of theirs mentioned at dinner that she'd recently been blown away by a poem a guy sent her. She showed the text around. Do I need to go on? It turned out to be the same poem, same guy. He copied and pasted to the two women (if not more). Stacy couldn't believe it. He sounded so sincere! She took another look and saw that there wasn't anything specific to her in his poem. It was generic. He might not have written it, for all she knew.

Why did it play by text when it wouldn't have in person? When a man lies to your face or on the phone, you subconsciously pick up the clues. He looks down and to the right. His voice goes up an octave. Even if you don't know why your liar-radar switches on, the bleeping is loud and clear. With a text, however, he isn't weirdly avoiding eye contact. He doesn't clear his throat suspiciously, or shrug, or shuffle his feet. You have nothing to go on but the text.

As far as body language goes, texting is blind.

lisa

A guy promised to call and then didn't. He said he couldn't call for whatever reason, like he couldn't get to a phone, or he lost your number. He couldn't get to a phone, despite there being a landline in nearly every room he entered? If he really cared, he could hunt down a pay phone on the street (that would be true love). Every person he came into contact with was most likely holding a phone. His computer at home and work were Internet accessible. If he lost your number, he could have gone old-school and sent an e-mail, a Facebook message, a tweet, etc. He could have texted a mutual friend for your number and had it in seconds.

Now, we all know the "couldn't get in touch" excuse is completely absurd. That might've been legit a long time ago in a galaxy far, far away.

In the old days (aka the '90s), he could blow you off, say, two ways. Now, there are eighteen forms of rejection. We feel obliged to go through each and every form, just to re-re-re-reconfirm that he's not into us.

Texting makes lying easier, on both sides.

It also makes accepting the truth a lot harder. "

so he's into me . . .
even if he types little white lies?

Bro consensus: The old saying is that any intelligent person will lie to get himself out of trouble. But the real truth, as we all know, is that by lying, you get yourself into trouble. According to one argument, he wouldn't lie if he didn't care. According to the other, he'd be honest if he respected you. Both are true, both are lies. There is no official Truth in Texting policy on the books. But if he's fast and loose with the truth online, he is way into you.*

brian

Guys think they can get away with everything. So they lie and say they're in one place, even if their actual location is accessible on Foursquare or via Facebook check-in. That is, if he's stupid enough to

---

* A lie.

drop a pin. Checking in and telling everyone where you are when you hope to keep your location on the DL? It's just plain idiotic. I don't know anyone who uses either of those apps. Men like their privacy. They don't want someone watching them, or catching them in a lie. This is why a lot of guys won't add girls on Facebook. If I didn't want to hang out with her on any given night, why should that be an issue? Well, it would be if she saw me post a photo with a friend at a bar after I'd told her I wasn't feeling well. Social networks have made the gentle rejection impossible. You can't let a girl down easy anymore. There's no "something came up" and getting the benefit of the doubt.

An outright lie is one thing. Saying, "I did not have sex with that woman," while she's lying in the bed with you is a bold-faced lie. But to some guys, giving a girl a cover story instead of a long-winded explanation (that might hurt her feelings) isn't really lying. It's better than the absolute truth, as in, "I'm not in the mood to see you tonight." That could block his chances with her when he *is* in the mood. It's easier to say, "I'm staying in," than to deal with repercussions. Some nights you want to see a girl. Sometimes you'd rather hang with your friends. Nothing personal!

But girls often take it that way. Hence, the harmless little white text.

Now, the trouble starts when you get busted. The lie you told to avoid pressure and an argument suddenly turns into a HUGE fight about trust and honesty. Guys never think they'll be found out. They just shovel lies on top of lies to get out from under, while digging themselves in deeper.

It's my opinion that girls let guys off the hook way too often. It sounds horrible, especially when put like that. When there's no defined relationship, men don't want it to seem like they are putting other priorities over you or have to answer to a girl they're not committed to. But they do want the girl to believe she's number one anyway. The lies are really just guys hedging their bets and choosing the path of perceived least resistance. ""

kenny

Brian, so true. "Path of perceived least resistance." Girls know when you're lying. They can sense it. They might let you off, but they know what's what. I'm not talking about any Text Sixth Sense. It's that guys' lies are obvious! A guy says he's staying in but tweets that he's at a bar. It's just dumb. Men might think women are as stupid as they are. They honestly think that they won't be found out.

Why lie at all? Because he has something to hide. If he's lying about going out, it probably means he's looking for another girl or has already found one. Depending on the relationship, it's okay to talk to him about it. If you've been together for a while, bring it up and make sure it doesn't happen again. If this is a new guy, lying is obviously a bad sign. Forget him and move on to the next one.

I also think some men *want* to get busted, just to prove to a girl that no one can put reins on him or tell him what to do. That guy is a Player and a dick. Beware.

jared

Everyone gets caught lying sometimes. If a girl calls him out on it, a guy denies, denies, denies, and more often than not, she lets it go.

I have a theory about why more women don't confront a guy with the damning evidence about his lies. They're so afraid of getting the "crazy girl" or "uptight girl" label that they give him a pass. If he blatantly lied, he deserves to be called on it. Girls have to get over being afraid to be crazy. Who isn't crazy? Everybody is a little insane. It's just a matter of levels of insanity. "

want

A guy who . . .

✳ Tells the truth.

✳ Has the decency/brains not to flaunt his lie on Facebook.

✳ Wouldn't think of insulting your intelligence with denials, just admits the truth when confronted, and begs on his knees for forgiveness.

✳ Would never ever, ever mess with your bathroom scale, even as a prank. That shit is NOT FUNNY.

do not want

A liar who . . .

✳ Lies.

✳ Cheats.

✳ Steals.

✳ Forges.

✳ Embezzles.

* Gaslights.

* Engages in any other form of criminal and personal deception.

autocorrect

The day might come when Honest Jane has to dance around what, in most circles, is known as the truth. Yes, women also lie. At least we do it with more skill and regret than men! If you do have something to hide and must fib, follow the Liar's Playbook. Stay as close to the truth as possible. Cover your tracks. Get an alibi. And avoid the subject in future conversations. If you feel an overriding urge to confess, do it face-to-face. Nothing could be more chickenshit than texting your contrition. It'll read as another falsehood.

the memo

Texting is made for liars because phones are machines. Messages are a way to communicate, but they're not a means to connect on a human level. You have to look someone in the eye to do that. What someone would never lie about F2F, they would blithely type via text in a heartbeat.

(14)

he booty texted

He texted after midnight and wants to
see you right away. Does this mean the
love train is on track?

the context

The Booty Text, similar to the traditional Booty Call, is what
happens when a guy (or a woman) has had a little too much to
drink and starts thinking about the black hole of his romantic
life. He feels sad and alone. Instead of just going to sleep, he
scrolls through his contact list, searching for someone to connect with. A name pops up, and a text is sent to an old flame,
asking her for comfort and companionship and a chance to
forget the loneliness of human existence, if only for a little
while.

Or the guy just wants to get laid.

the subtext

carrie

One HeTexted user sent us a text from a guy that read, "We ended things badly. I really need to make it right between us. Can you come to my apartment at 3 A.M., just to talk?"

The girl asked us, "I know it sounds like a Booty Text. But we did end it badly, and he does owe me an apology. I really love this guy. What should I do?"

Oh, girl. If you don't know what to do about that, you really need to start reading this book again at page one. He's luring you in with "just to talk" nonsense. Maybe he does want to "talk," for about three minutes—before the lunge. Hey, if you're lonely too and are fine with a hookup, by all means, go ahead. Have your no-strings-attached fun. But make no mistake about it. This is not about love or reviving a dead relationship.

The Booty Text is a dare. Will you jump when he calls?

We hope your answer is, "How high . . . do you think I am? There's not enough tequila in the world, you idiot."

lisa

I have yet to meet a woman who, upon receiving a Booty Text, thinks, "Yay! I get to be used for sex and then kicked to the curb! So psyched!"

No, she thinks, "He does like me after all."

If your friend received the Booty Text, you'd recognize the emotional manipulation immediately. But when you're involved, it's harder to see what's really happening. The hope is that, if he's thinking about you at 3 A.M., he cares. He's tossing and turning, tortured by thoughts of you. Driven to insomnia over his passion and/or regret. His midnight (or later) text can only mean that your relationship has a shot after all.

I can't say that it does or doesn't. But I can say that it's rare for a Booty Text to come from a place of love and respect. Think about it. If you sent a Booty Text, would it be to the guy you truly loved and admired, or would it be to the doormat who would show up on command and then disappear without an argument?

so he's into me . . .
if he sends a late-night text to hook up?

Bro consensus: He couldn't be more into you—until dawn. And then, it's like the two of you have never met.

brian

"Just to talk" at 3 A.M., really? Hey, no better time to have a serious conversation. He's using your desire to be in a relationship to get you into bed. And then, later on, when the girl says she thought it meant something, he'll say, "But it was just a Booty Text." The method implies a casual hookup. Not binding romantic involvement. If she didn't know that, it's because she fell into a "what if" fantasy. He will feel free to flip the tables and say, "I thought you understood. Now get out."

Guys can be heartless. In a certain frame of mind, they will try anything to get a girl to come over. If she likes the guy, a woman will find a way to attach romantic significance to that. She can read into it in a million ways, but the only meaning that actually makes sense gets lost. If the girl refuses to leave in the morning, gets clingy, or expects something out of it, he'll regret this spur-of-the-moment decision to text. It might be karma coming back to him. But he won't see it that way.

Nov 1, 2013, 12:54 PM

Thanks for last night I had fun

Nov 1, 2013, 12:55 PM

So I woke up this morning and remember nothing that happened.

Nov 1, 2013, 12:55 PM

Really?

Nov 1, 2013, 12:55 PM

Yeah really

That's it, DB. If you pretend it never happened, maybe she'll go away.

kenny

I wouldn't look for anything serious with a Booty Texter. Most guys send a Booty Text spontaneously; it's not the complex thought process that girls make it out to be. In terms of a relationship, it probably isn't the best sign. If the girl responds to the text and actually shows up at 3 A.M., she can expect to hear for him again—next time he's drunk, bored, and it's way past closing time.

Come clean my house, have sex with me, and then take off. Cool??

jared

I would be lying if I said I have never sent a text after 1 A.M. Responses have ranged from a girl saying, "Be right there," to no reply, to a girl never texting me again, to a non-answer after the fact, like, "I fell asleep and didn't see your text." The Booty Text is a dick move, for sure. But if you get positive responses for being a dick, you keep being one.

I'm not going to marry the hookup girl. That's not what the future holds for us. If you've been on two dates and the only time you hear from the guy is late at night, he thinks of you in one way only. It's casual. It's not going to change and become something completely different. Booty Texting is not how people fall in love. Not to say it can never happen. But if you are the casual-hookup girl, if you take that call, you're setting a precedent.

want

A text that . . .

✳ Arrives by Wednesday at 3 P.M. to ask you out for dinner that weekend.

* Is clear and concise.

* Asks if you need help salting your driveway to get your car out for the date.

* Is a follow-up the day after your date, thanking you and asking you out again.

do not want

A BT that . . .

* Comes in after all the bars have closed for the night.

* Is the text version of slurred speech.

* Is a follow-up a month later at 3 A.M. that denies any knowledge of your last hookup.

autocorrect

If you receive a Booty Text, the only possible reply is, "I'll pass. But thanks for nothing!"

the memo

* If you've been in a relationship for two years and he texts late at night to say, "I need you now," that's kind of sweet and romantic.

✳ If it's after two dates, that's sick and twisted. You're not his dog. You don't come on command. Not even for a Scooby Snack.

✳ When in doubt, reply, "Text me when you're sober."

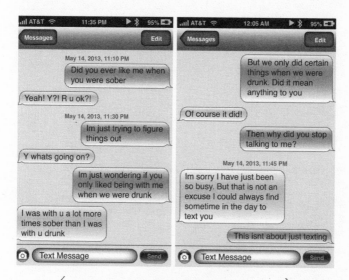

There should be designated texter laws. Don't drink and text, people! It's dangerous enough out there.

(15)

he ended it

relationship live to text again?

the context

Stopped texting, "liking" your updates, retweeting, commenting, favoriting, all the digital "-ings" out there. You suspect something's going on. He's probably really busy or dealing with some other stuff. The last time you heard from him, he said something about things being complicated or not a good time. He might've mentioned some ex-girlfriend's resurfacing or that he had to leave town. He could have cut it off, in so many words. It had to be temporary, though. When the two of you were together, you really connected. You felt it. You're sure he felt it. He might be scared of his own feelings. Despite the signs, you know he'll turn up again at some point, sooner rather than later.

the subtext

carrie

Wake up and smell the cold, hard truth (which, unfortunately, does not smell like coffee). When a man falls off a digital cliff, he is not lying broken and bloody at the base of an actual cliff. He's somewhere else, living his life, thinking of you fondly, perhaps, but probably not much at all. You might've gone out for five minutes, five months, or five years. But when a guy is done, he's pretty much done. When the flirty texts and in-joke comments stop, it's over.

Ideally, there would have been a long conversation and a trial separation. The breakup would have been your call, or a mutual decision. A guy just pulling the plug without talking first is BS. You deserve more than that. You are owed an explanation and an apology. But it isn't an ideal world. Guys far prefer the "cut and run" to the "yell and cry." I'm sure you're an awesome, lovely girl, and he was a total toolbag who was lucky to be with you. You haven't done anything wrong. As much as he should be begging on his knees for you to love him, he's chosen to end it. Unfortunately, in a relationship, if one person wants out, you both have to put down your devices and go your separate ways.

The unique problem of dumping in the digital age: We get so used to the texts and the comments that when they stop or turn cruel and dismissive, it's a shock. You have your entire text history to scroll through for the first sign of problems. You have evidence of everything he'd written before. You can stalk him a thousand ways, which keeps him on your mind. Either party can send a text in two seconds that they'll regret in three seconds. (At least dialing someone's phone and waiting for the answering machine gave you a chance to change your mind and hang up.) It's all so immediate, your brain and heart can't keep up with the fast changes in how you're supposed to think and feel. It's disconcerting and confusing. We just can't be sure what's happening or what to believe.

lisa

Again, the tone of a text can be left open to interpretation. He might text, "Let's break up," but if it's after a long text chain of jokes and banter, should you take that seriously?

You can hear the truth in a voice and see it on a face. But adding a frowny-face emoji just won't cut it. Since men will avoid a scene whenever possible, they prefer to end it via text. They don't have to be on the other end of the phone or across from you at a table. They just type the words and wash their hands of you. It's irresistible for them and reprehensible to you.

A lot of users at HeTexted ask how they can win a man back via text. Well, you can't make him like you, no matter how clever your messages. And you shouldn't have to force it like this. Although it feels like a defeat to retreat gracefully and never text him again, you win by keeping your cool. This is another very clear case of Put the Phone Down. You'll only confirm his decision and possibly push him to be meaner to you. He's the asshole—but don't be the asshole-enabler.

so he's into me . . .
if he blows me off via text?

Bro consensus: Not sure if he's dumping you via text? When in doubt, the answer is YES. So, no, he's not into you anymore.

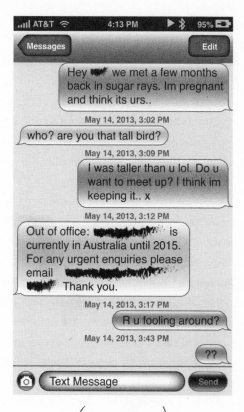

.ııll AT&T 🛜   4:13 PM   ▶ ✻   95% 🔋

Messages   **Edit**

Hey ▰▰ we met a few months back in sugar rays. Im pregnant and think its urs..

May 14, 2013, 3:02 PM

who? are you that tall bird?

May 14, 2013, 3:09 PM

I was taller than u lol. Do u want to meet up? I think im keeping it.. x

May 14, 2013, 3:12 PM

Out of office: ▰▰▰▰▰▰ is currently in Australia until 2015. For any urgent enquiries please email ▰▰▰▰▰▰▰▰ ▰▰▰ Thank you.

May 14, 2013, 3:17 PM

R u fooling around?

May 14, 2013, 3:43 PM

??

🄾   Text Message   Send

(The "Last Word")

brian

Dumping someone by text is one of the most cowardly things that you could do. It shows the guy has no backbone and is too immature to say what he wants. However, this ONLY applies to people in relationships.

If people are just casually dating and have only gone on a few dates, especially if you've never hooked up, then you don't owe the person a long explanation. You can just say, "I don't think it's working," and leave it at that. Unless the person is really dense, that sends a strong enough message.

Not responding, however, is a different story. It's not nice. But—you can't always be nice when dating. Niceness leads people on. Sometimes, in casual dating or when you hook up too soon, it goes south really quickly. The guy realizes it's not what he wants or he just loses interest. It's easier for him to just not reply to texts. He doesn't have to do anything and isn't in danger of leading you on. He also never has to say, "I don't like you." A guy will do just about anything to avoid that conversation. It might end in tears, which is unbearable.

From a guy's perspective, it's less hurtful to drop off the side of the earth and never reply, than to tell you specifically why he doesn't like you. Girls demand to know "Why???" He hesitates to tell you, because what he considers a flaw or a fault might be fine to another guy. He might be turned off by your donkey laugh. Another guy might find it charming. I wouldn't want to make someone self-conscious about the one thing that another man might fall head-over-heels in love with. If there is no future in a relationship, why go there? You won't see each other again. Who cares what he thinks? For the sake of future relationships? As I just said, each person is different. It just doesn't matter what turned off one person if someone else won't mind, or might like the "flaw."

I've been in that situation. I was casually dating a girl and started seeing a less than pleasant side to her. She got demanding and kept asking to go on dates. I never gave her any encouragement. I always had plans or said the polite, "Can't make it." She refused to hear what I was clearly telling her. Not interested. (Ladies, a guy knows that an attitude will only get worse over time. If you come on strong in the beginning, he'll assume you'll be Godzilla within months.) What bothered me the most: I wasn't what she wanted, obviously. But she kept demanding we get together. Oh, I was also really annoyed by her using emojis to convey real emotions. It was just weird. Smileys are one thing. But using the angry face to convey actual anger is just childish. Incorporating emojis into any serious conversation automatically diminishes it. You lose credibility, and the tone can be misconstrued.

It might seem like a cop-out to give a one-sentence "It's not working" or just not respond. But "why" is a trap to be avoided, in the asking or answering. ”

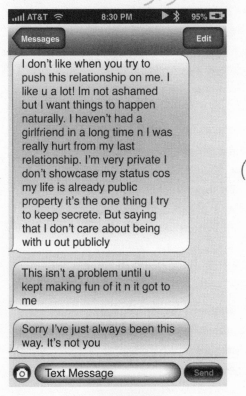

I don't like when you try to push this relationship on me. I like u a lot! Im not ashamed but I want things to happen naturally. I haven't had a girlfriend in a long time n I was really hurt from my last relationship. I'm very private I don't showcase my status cos my life is already public property it's the one thing I try to keep secrete. But saying that I don't care about being with u out publicly

This isn't a problem until u kept making fun of it n it got to me

Sorry I've just always been this way. It's not you

(The "It's Not You." No kidding.

kenny

Dumping by text is the worst. There's no way around that. It's a cowardly act and potentially dangerous. We've had a HeTexted reader get broken up with by text in the car and then have a car accident because she was so shocked! Some guys will keep texting after the relationship ended for a variety of reasons:

* They're unsure about the breakup.

* They want to keep their options open.

* They're just used to texting you.

* They want to make sure that you're okay and not upset with them.

There is no good way to let a girl down by text. If the relationship is new, the "no response" is common. If the relationship is old, then I see a lot of standard "It's not working anymore" or "Let's take some time apart this summer because we'll be out of school" or something of that nature.

(The "Crazy Busy")

Longer-term relationships do require a better reason. The "crazy busy" excuse is a standard. Women tolerate it because they like men who work hard and are ambitious. Not saying he has to be rich and powerful. A street artist who is ambitious is more attractive to women than a guy who sits on his ass all day talking about the art he's going to make one day. So if he says, "I'm working my ass off," she might feel proud of him instead of seeing that he's making an excuse to blow her off. If he never wanted to see her again, he'd ignore her texts completely, or say horrible things like, "Not gonna happen." In the text window on the previous page, his blow-off seems particularly obnoxious because he admitted to the Do and Dash the night before. Two selfish acts within a twelve-hour window? This couple is not going to make it.

Almost without error, no matter how busy a guy is, if he's interested, he will find a way to see you. No one is too busy to send a text or write a quick message. So if he's not paying attention to you, he's not into you. Why is he keeping you on a string with excuses? Some guys are just like that. They like to have a Plan B, C, D, and E in place. Just make sure that his actions back up his sweet words.

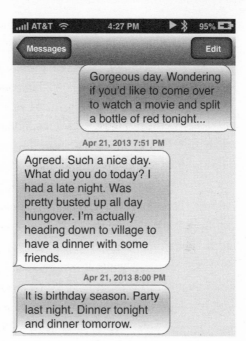

(The "No Reply Reply")

> Gorgeous day. Wondering if you'd like to come over to watch a movie and split a bottle of red tonight...

Apr 21, 2013 7:51 PM

> Agreed. Such a nice day. What did you do today? I had a late night. Was pretty busted up all day hungover. I'm actually heading down to village to have a dinner with some friends.

Apr 21, 2013 8:00 PM

> It is birthday season. Party last night. Dinner tonight and dinner tomorrow.

jared

I get a lot of girls who say, "We broke up, but he's still texting. I kind of want to get back with him. Does he still like me?" Think about his state of mind post-breakup. He used to text you a dozen times a day. Now there is a void. There was somebody you used to text, somebody you used to hug and hang out with. Now, that's all gone. Usually what we do to fill the void is go back to the person we just dumped to fill it, even though we may have had reasons for ending it in the first place. We don't care. We still want to get those texts every day.

I have dated girls for a year (but none for longer than that; my personal compulsion). There was nothing wrong with them. I just knew they were not the person for me. That's totally fine. No qualms about ending it. But then a week or so goes by and you think, *Holy shit. It's been awfully quiet. Why is it so quiet? No one is texting me.* I remember the back-and-forth all day with my recent ex, how much I miss that it's gone. So I might send her a text. If she asks me to get together, I dance around it. I don't want to get together with her. I just want to text her. "

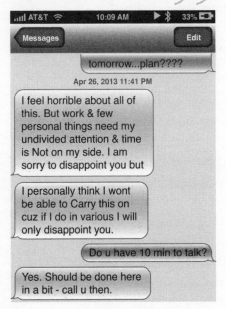

(The "I'm Not Worthy")

brian

A guy is only too happy to take the blame for a breakup if it means he won't have to upset her. It's the entire ethos behind "It's not you, it's me." The "I'm not worthy" blow-off strategy takes the same idea, but the guy amps up everything that's wrong with him, his lifestyle, his choices, his abilities, etc. The problem is, women are so forgiving, the approach might backfire. She might assure him she'll take him on, despite all of his many, many problems and flaws. If so, he'll have to change his approach and might get mean. So, women, if a guy tells you that he is a pathetic loser and will only disappoint you, TAKE HIM AT HIS WORD.

HE TEXTED ME THIS...

Dating for 5 months, he wanted to take things slow, so we are not boyfriend/girlfriend.

.ıll AT&T 📶   11:44 PM   ▶ ✳ 33% 🔋

Messages   Edit

That's good. Hopefully not too many trips up and down stairs.

I'm naked in bed thinking of you.

Barely made a dent

You're not one for sexy messages are you?

Nov. 19, 2012, 11:30 PM

Don't want to keep you up. Good night. Hope you get a good sleep and dogs don't wake you up before you have to get out of bed. Xox

(The "I Got Nothing")

Night night young lady. Sweet dreams.

Text Message Send

...SO NOW I'M WONDERING?

Am I wasting my time?

brian

This might seem shocking, if not downright revolutionary, but yes, guys do get tired sometimes. You heard it here first. Even the offer of some grade-A action on a silver plate couldn't motivate us to wake up or change what we're doing when exhausted. Sometimes not wanting to see a girl makes it easier to say no. But if he's a jerk about it, he's blowing you off. Otherwise, he'd be careful not to upset you for the next time you make an offer.

HE TEXTED ME THIS...

.ıll AT&T 📶   11:15 PM   ▶ ✳ 86% 🔋

Messages   Edit

> No response?

I'm thinking last night was a mistake

> You said you guys had broken up!

It's complicated, and we've been talking again. I really appreciate you not telling anyone. Ok?

📷 (Text Message)   Send

(The "Ex-File")

As crappy as it is, stuff like that (the Ex-Files above) happens. After a guy gets out of a relationship, his first hookup often brings back old memories and emotions about his ex. It can drive him back into the arms of his ex, a cycle that can happen several times (wash, rinse, repeat).

kenny

If the ex-girlfriend really is in the picture, guys use this breakup strategy as a way of hedging their bets. He's playing multiple hands. He might like the ex more than you. He might've gotten caught up with you and changed his mind in the cold light of morning. He might just want to stay on friendly terms with you while he sorts things out with the ex. He might be making it all up to keep you on standby. Women seem more accepting of this strategy because it's kind of sweet and forgivable that he still loves the ex. That's what makes it a good ploy. If he surfaces six months later, he might just be cycling you back in. But you think fondly of him for being a romantic. "

(The "It's All a Blur")

jared

Guys are willing to say, "Screw it, there are other fish in the sea," but women tend to cling to relationships, even after they've gone bad. Why do they do it? I have a theory: Women are actually oracles. They can see a future in just about any relationship! They've seen it from Date One and wrote a story about it before anything actually happened.

I'm at the age where everyone I know is getting engaged and married. If I go to one more wedding where the maid of honor gets up and makes a speech that says, "The bride told me after their first date that the groom was the man of her dreams," I will blow my brains out. I think women say, "He's the One," after half of all of their first dates, just in case it turns out that way and the bridesmaids can make their speeches. Does that sound cynical? The odds just don't justify every bride knowing every groom was the One, unless she hedged her bets. We can't be shooting a thousand percent on this.

I honestly believe that girls get more excited about their story than about the man himself. I've been in a relationship where the girl posted updates about us constantly along the lines of "Jared and I did this over the weekend. He's so sweet!" "Jared. Best. Boy-friend. Evah." "Spending the night at Jared's #futureroomies?" I read the updates, and I kept thinking, *Who's this Jared guy she's talking about?* I met her for a hot dog on the corner, and she posted, "Lunch with my boy." She turned the relationship into something it wasn't, and me into a romantic hero, which (let's be honest) I'm not. I felt like she was using me to paint a pretty picture for her friends. None of them care about the reality. They just want a romantic story too.

For this reason, when a guy ends it, women often say, "I didn't see it coming." They were living in the fantasy future of the relationship, not the present reality. When a guy gets the hint that a girl is making plans for their future, a warning light flickers on his emotional dashboard. The deeper she goes into her fantasy version of the relationship, the more he wants to get out of it. He makes his breakup noises, cancels plans, ignores texts; she refuses to read the message he's sending, loud and clear. Subtle hints don't work. He has to break out the big guns. And STILL she doesn't get it. On HeTexted, we have girls asking, "Is he dumping me?" after a guy sent a text that read, "Let's break up."

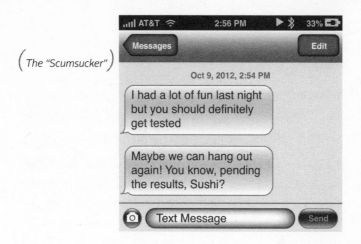

(*The "Scumsucker"*)

Oct 9, 2012, 2:54 PM

I had a lot of fun last night but you should definitely get tested

Maybe we can hang out again! You know, pending the results, Sushi?

want

A send-off that . . .

* Is clear enough that your five-year-old niece could read it and say, "You are so dumped."

* If it has to be by text instead of by voice, face-to-face, or via FaceTime, it should be dignified and respectful. No emojis, abbreves, winks, or "hahaha." Definitely no links, photos, or attachments. Although such a respectful ending might make you want him all the more. Which gets to . . .

* Makes you hate him a little bit. Let it be clear, dignified, and a bit obnoxious.

do not want

A blow-off that . . .

✳ Is as floppy and limp as you will tell your girlfriends your ex was. It might seem strange to men, but a hard "no" is easier on a woman's self-esteem than a soft "I don't know."

✳ Lingers. After the breakup, don't keep texting each other. Forget being "friends" (non-FB variety) for at least a year. Then, a text out of the blue might be a welcome throwback.

top ten ways he's saying he's over you without saying he's over you

If a guy texts any of the following lines, you are well and truly dumped.

10. "Big news! I'm moving to Cuba."

9. "I don't believe in monogamy."

8. "I'll never love a woman as much as I love my dog."

7. "Can't make it to your party. Got a hot date."

6. "I'm not really attracted to _____ [your hair color here] girls."

5. "Yup, crazy busy for the foreseeable future."

4. "Your new lingerie. LOL. Get a refund."

3. "I'll pass on the sext."

2. "Lose my number."

1. "It's not you. It's my opinion of you."

autocorrect

How to handle yourself if you're the dumpee? Unless he's the father of your child, don't fight for a man who doesn't want you. Don't go nuts with text messages, especially hassling him about not texting you. That's just annoying, and he already doesn't want to pursue the relationship further. I'd move on to the next guy and get your texting under control.

Although we see no reason you can't take one parting shot.

(*This girl is our hero!*)

If you're the dumper? Follow the Golden Rule. Dump others as you would have them dump you. If you'd like to get a short, sweet, honest text, that's what you should send. If you would prefer a phone call or a face-to-face encounter, then act accordingly. No matter how messy things get, if your conscience is clean, you'll have no regrets.

the memo

Brian's Text Enders Guidelines:

❋ Everything you say via text can and will be used against you. It makes your words permanent and easy to share with the world.

❋ If you're in an established relationship with someone, you owe it to each other to say you want to end things over the phone or in person—not by text.

❋ If you're casually dating or hooking up with someone, then no one owes anyone anything. Stop communicating if you want, or text that you don't want to continue. Either way, the result is the same. The other person feels hurt, but will get over it.

❋ Don't ask "Why?" What do you gain with the knowledge that a man you'll never see again thinks you chew loudly? Do you really care what he thinks anyway? No. So give up the need to hear a laundry list of what some jerk thinks is "wrong with you," and know someone else will see it as "all right."

✳ Don't beg. Ever. He won't care, you'll look pathetic, and you'll feel pathetic having him witness your desperation. Don't beg for dates. Don't beg for attention. You won't get it, and you're just going to drive the guy away. If he wants you, there won't be a need to beg.

facebook breakups

Facebook is one of the worst things that ever happened to dating and relationships. People stalk each other, get suspicious if their significant other gets a new Friend or has someone of the opposite sex write on their wall, for example. Breakups can be brutal in the public realm that is FB. A simple status change (and the sympathetic comments from his Friends, especially the female ones) can throw you into a tizzy for a week. That's seven days you'll never get back. Seven days of doubling down on agony. Although breakup pain can be strangely addicting (we're all masochists when freshly single), it's healthier to move on as quickly as possible. You can't heal if every time you go on Facebook is like ripping off the scab all over again. With skin infections in mind, we urge you to:

Unfriend immediately. It's the only way to ensure you won't get jealous or stalk the other person. It helps you manage your emotions not to see his updates or comments from his friends. Over time, your romantic feelings will dissipate. You'll focus on your friends and your life, not on him, and realize (much sooner than you thought) that you weren't right for each other anyway. You might hate him. Hate can be useful for analyzing the deeper emotion underneath it, like your fear for the future or whatever. Take some pleasure in throwing him off your Wall, and then let hate guide you to self-awareness, not more useless anger at a man who is no longer in your life.

Put his friends on the Restricted List. Friends report what's going on to their friends. It's second-degree stalking, and just as unhealthy as first-degree. It might be worse, since other people get drawn into it. You can always take them off Restricted later. But for a few months, circle your wagons.

Friends don't let friends hack their Wall. A friend of ours Unfriended her ex and his friends. But this former couple had mutual friends from college, including her BFF. She knew her bestie's password and logged on as her to lurk her ex's Wall. If you haven't gotten this memo: Hack kills. If this happens more than twice, ask your friend to change her password for her sake and yours. And put out the warning to your other friends not to let you "borrow" their phones.

Update your status. Just do it, and be done with it. Since you've Unfriended him, his status update won't anger or aggravate you, because you won't see it. You won't see the "likes" and comments about it. You won't know anything. You'll only bask in the sympathy and support from your friends—and field new offers.

(16)

he loves you

He texted the three little words! "Bring
home Doritos." You replied, "K." And
then he said, "I love you." So does he
really and truly love you, or DORITOS??
Or both?? (Or neither.)

the context

Texting any words of endearment is dubious, unfortunately.
FB friends will comment on our Wall, "Luv ya! Take care!
XOXOXOXOXOX" if you update that you got caught in a
rainstorm. You'd think so much love would be reserved for
hurricanes. The "love" online ranges free, like organic chick-
ens, with roughly the same-size heart. People routinely say
they love people they know only on Twitter or FB. So if a man
texts, "I love you," does that count? What would happen if
you dared to say it back IRL?

(*Good question.*)

the subtext

lisa

Obviously, those are loaded words that get slung around a lot in a casual context online. But you don't want to hear them that way—especially for the first time. You want to hear them from his lips, moments after he's kissed you, as the candlelight flickers. Or maybe that's just me. I want to feel the love and see it in his eyes. The emotion simply cannot be conveyed by text. It's an insufficient forum for such a major moment in a relationship. We have users ask us all the time, "He texted it, but does he really feel it?" Only you can be the judge of his sincerity. But texting the words and slapping a few dozen heart emojis at the end does not convince me of a man's love.

Remember: Women fall easy, and men fall hard. For a man to say, "I love you," is a huge deal. If he sends a message of love by text? As I've learned to say in New York, "Meh."

so he's into me . . .
if he texts, "i love you"?

Bro Consensus: He's into you if he *says*, "I love you."

kenny

Using heavy, loaded language in a casual medium? You can apply the upside-down rule of Internet communications. If he says, "I love you"—or "love ya" or "lurve u," or any of a dozen variations—on Facebook, he means, "We're friends." Come on. You must have friends who post, "Oh my God, I love you guys. You're the best," heart, heart, heart. Everyone on Facebook loves each other, and hearts overflow, and they're all the very, very best. You can see where I'm going. It might not be the forum for deep, genuine emotion. Sometimes, yes. But usually? Nope. It's kind of shocking, how easily people spout their love on FB. The sheer volume of flowing love could drown us all. I wish that many people loved me in real life!

If he really felt deep romantic love for you, he just wouldn't bury it in a comment on an update about missing your morning train. He'd burst out with it when he was with you and couldn't hold it in for one more second. Or he'd set the stage, to acknowledge it as the relationship milestone it is.

If he really feels it, he won't type it. Some things are meant to be said in person.

Now, if he did pull a chump move and say, "I love you," by text for the first time for real, and you didn't reciprocate because you assumed it was just the "heart, heart" treatment, what then? He'll be embarrassed. He'll worry that he's the one who wants more—an awkward, vulnerable position to be in. If he starts acting strange, cut him some slack and ask, "Did you mean it?" BUT ONLY IF you're not ready to say it back. If you don't feel the same way, asking him if he loves you for real would be rubbing salt in an open wound. You don't have to say it back if you're not comfortable. But once one person says it and the other doesn't reciprocate, the expiration date on that relationship is stamped in ink. **"**

brian

Every relationship is different. Every couple has their own style. But I do believe that a couple that only expresses their feelings through a digital device is missing something important. To really show your feelings and affection, the perfect way for him to say, "I love you," is to your face. To bring out my sappy side, I believe in saying, "I love you," loud and often. My girlfriend and I are in a long-distance relationship, so I make sure she hears it plenty when I'm with her.

There is obviously more meaning in saying it face-to-face than in hearing it over the phone. Typing it online isn't a terrible thing. I have no problem texting it or Skyping it. I'm beginning to think that I am really sappy. What did the other Bros say? Never mind.

I don't want to know.

You shouldn't type, "I love you," in a text until you've said it face-to-face. If a guy actually did love you, he would sack up despite his nerves, go out there, and say what has to be said. If you don't reciprocate, he won't say it again. He will shut that sucker down. Now, you could give him an explanation—you're not ready, etc.—and that might keep the relationship alive for a while. He'll put in some more time. But once the *L*-bomb gets dropped and it goes unanswered for more than a few days, it's essentially a slap in the face to whichever person got emotionally invested in the other.

jared

Remember, it's so much easier to say things via text than it is to say them in person. I wouldn't believe anything that someone texts me. He might text such things because he knows it gets you to bed a little bit quicker.

If he says it in person, the tone in the room changes. He sees your reaction, the look on your face. He hopes you say it back. There's a lot of pressure. But if he texts, the pressure is reduced. You might not reply. He'll be hurt, but it's a lot easier to take if you're not giving him sad eyes. Take the "I love you" text for what it is: a warm-up. He might be testing the waters.

Don't text, "I love you," to him on a feed-back mission. If the subject makes him feel uncomfortable, he'll never mention it or will pretend he didn't even see it. To test his reaction for real, you have to say it to him. He can make excuses about a text. There are no excuses in the room.

"I love you" is one example of text declarations that you can't take as the literal truth. I don't care how sweet it is, how nice it is, how sincere it sounds. With texts, you just can't believe what you read—good or bad. A text offense can be written off as well, to some extent. I do think, in either case, that if the text is causing you serious distraction, you should bring it up in person to get a real take on it.

One of the many excuses women make for me is, "He can only write things. He can't say them." That's bullshit. Even shy men have to grow up at some point. If he won't grow up for you, then why bother with him? People are busy until they don't want to be. People are shy until they don't want to be. People have been falling in love for thousands and thousands of years before cell phones existed. How did a Shy Guy get away with not saying it in previous eras? He didn't. He eventually had to declare himself, or he lived alone and didn't get the chance to pass along his genes. It was his own damn fault.

A chump move to say it by text for the first time, but still sweet.

want

A man who ...

❋ Is a grown-ass man who can speak the words that need to be said.

❋ Is a lover. Not in the icky "lovah" sense. A lover can accept that love is a joy and a blessing.

❋ Is a fighter. He will do battle with his own demons, make

himself vulnerable to you by saying how he feels—that you are beautiful and wonderful and deserve to be told that every day.

do not want

A pseudo-man who . . .

✳ Is a quivering little boy who gets tongue-tied over three short, common words in the English language and resorts to typing them instead, or just uses a heart emoji.

✳ Is a hater. He hates deep emotions, commitments that threaten his freedom to play miniature golf or go deep-sea fishing or whatever doods do when they get laid, like, never.

✳ Is a slacker. He wouldn't take the time and trouble to wrestle with his demons, let alone slay them. It's too much effort to reassure a needy woman, so why bother, he thinks. Good luck to him in his bachelor apartment, with the roaches and the empty pizza boxes. Womankind won't miss him a smidge.

autocorrect

He texted, "I love you"? Our bros would have you do nothing. You can wait for him to text it again, but a dozen "I love you" texts still aren't equal to one spoken to your face. We think you could text reply, "What's that? I can't hear you? You'll have to speak up," after his tenth "I love you" text. Just to put the subject on the front burner.

If you make the mistake of texting, "I love you," and get

no response, you have to back-burner that in a major way. He might take it as seriously as we advised you to—meaning not at all—because a text is not a declaration. It could be a typo. It could be wild Internet exaggeration. But you did make a move. Now wait for him to send something back over the net. Until then, just turn down the heat and let it simmer back there. An alternative could be to downplay it by overusing the *L*-word. "Love that show!" "Love that restaurant!" etc. It could work. But that would be a bit fake. And we're all about keeping it (light, smart, precise, and . . .) REAL in texting.

the memo

Love is the point. It's the destination. It's the human connection we use our mechanical devices to make. It's the zero-steps-removed intimacy we crave. It's why we deal with all the confusion, ego bruising, and frustration of flirting, dating, texting, sexting, all of it, in the first place.

So why on earth or cyberspace would you accept a declaration of love—LOVE, ladies, the biggie, the reason for everything, the ultimate joy—by text?

Well, you won't. If you learn anything from this entire book, it's to take nothing less than you deserve. Every woman deserves a lot. To keep her privacy and dignity. To be treated with kindness and respect. Mostly, we deserve honesty and bravery.

If a man loves you, really loves you, he won't need his iPhone to say it. He will tell you.

And then, when the kissing and crying are over and he falls asleep, go ahead and update your status to "HAPPY!!!!!!!!!!!"

signing off

And here we come to the end. A few final thoughts about dating in the digital age from all of us.

 lisa
You would think that now that we're all so accessible and reachable it would make things go more smoothly. But it just adds to the ambiguities. Communication is not the same as connection. Since we communicate so much—via texting, FB, e-mails, etc.—girls (and guys) assume that we're also connecting. It's so easy to interpret a text in the most hopeful way possible and create whatever little narrative you like, instead of seeing the relationship as it really is. Just because you text him regularly doesn't mean you're actually in his life, or that it's a real relationship.

In my own real life, HeTexted has been a great weeding-out process. Only the very brave text me! And when they do, it's never ambiguous, just very straightforward and to the point. Sometimes I get e-mails now with the subject line "He E-Mailed," which is kind of cute, and kind of . . . not really that romantic, but hey. I'll take them. I'm still not going out with anyone. (Hello, New York! Hello, London! Hello, anywhere! Text me!), and I intend to keep this book on my night table to make sure I don't forget what we wrote. HeTexted has been an awesome adventure for Carrie and me. More than anything else, I'm just really grateful that we get to have so much fun every day, doing what my girlfriends still spend way too much time doing already. Also! My bet is that a Bro wedding with one of the users is just a matter of time (but probably not Jared . . .).

jared

Being a "Bro" for HeTexted has taught me a number of things:

1. Girls write very long and in-depth questions, and girls notice everything.

2. Guys are blissfully aloof (guilty as charged).

3. Everyone is hooking up. No version of religion or God is stopping this generation from sending pictures of their genitalia to each other.

4. The most important thing I've learned is how easy it is to text. Not easy because Verizon has great service, but because it's just easy. It's easy to text your feelings and your emotions, because there's very little risk. You don't have to see a person's reaction to "I like you" or "I just farted." You can just click off a text, press Send, and then turn the phone over like it never happened. We've become numb to the power of words. The number of girls getting texts about a guy's feelings but never spending real quality time in their physical presence is pretty shocking.

That's why we have to look at texting as a tool. Is the person you're texting using this tool to achieve a goal (more time with you), or are they just tooling around? The answer to that question is not to confuse hope with a plan. What's the difference? Well, I hope to see a lot of girls naked. But I plan a dinner date with one in particular. Hoping he likes you but is too busy to respond is not a plan. Push him for action and jump ship if he doesn't make a move. Take every text one tenth as seriously as you would an F2F conversation. Don't send nip pics. That's your plan.

brian

Chances are you're going to get involved with the wrong person at one point or another. Those experiences can help you build your perception of what's out there and, more importantly, who you are and what you want out of a relationship. You can't force something to happen if the other person doesn't want the same thing. Rather than scramble after someone who doesn't reciprocate your feelings, take a step back. You can't change who you are. That's a good thing. Someone out there wants just what you have to offer. What the digital age offers is a chance to quickly learn about someone so you don't waste time pursuing the wrong person. You have the opportunity to get to know someone halfway around the world (or down the block) with a few taps on your phone.

For me, I learned what I wanted through trial and error and by observing others and hearing about their issues. HeTexted helped me understand how simple miscommunication could wreak havoc on a potential relationship. When I started talking to a girl in a different state, it began solely through text messages. I knew the weight each text carried and that there could be so much room for interpretation if I wasn't clear. The clearest form of communication, however, is going beyond words and showing how you feel by taking action. I went to visit her the first chance I got, and the months of getting to know each other via text paid off. Thanks to the myriad of communication methods at my fingertips, I was able to pursue someone who seemed right from a distance and confirmed that indeed she was. I was able to make it work, and things between us keep getting better and better. For us, texting did open a door. But we had to walk through it.

kenny

Finding the right person has always been a fun and difficult process, and digital communication hasn't made it any easier. However, remember that through all the miscommunication and confusing moments, things that should work themselves out always do in the end. Maybe it's not with this guy, or at this exact moment, but if you're true to yourself and stay positive, you'll end up in a relationship that makes you happy. Good luck out there!

carrie

So we've hit you over the head from eighteen different directions, begging you to think before you hit Send. We've explained why a picture is never just a picture, and why you're probably not going to like the reasoning behind a late-night text. But what we didn't dwell on (with good reason) is all of the fluffy stuff. The giddy Facebook chats that keep you up until 3 A.M. and the texts that *do* result in successful first dates. We're here to tell it like it is, but it's also probably important to remind you that with the bad will, eventually, come the good.

In a letter I gave to my husband on the morning of our wedding day, I started off with the exact words of his very first text to me. The words weren't fancy. They didn't have any kind of poetic tone to them. But they were mine—ours, really—and they were the beginning of what would eventually lead me down the aisle. It did occur to me how weird it was that I was starting such a significant letter with such a seemingly insignificant gesture, but I stuck with it. Because every time I think about them, even after the figurative and literal honeymoon, they still make my stomach drop. How's that for technology?

acknowledgments

Where would we be without our Bros? One million thank-yous to Jared Freid, Kenny Kline, and Brian McDermott. And a special thank-you to Tim Gough, the Original Bro. Val Frankel, we owe you our firstborn. We were lucky to have you. Thanks to our editors, Jeremie Ruby Strauss and Emilia Pisani, for always talking us off the ledge. To the HeTexted community, for making this book what it is. And to our early investors, for seeing what most couldn't.